3 1833 0075

D0941648

# FLEET ADMIRAL

The Story of William F. Halsey

*Westminster Press Books by*

Lawrence A. Keating

Junior Miler
Runner-Up
Wrong-Way Neelen
Fleet Admiral

# FLEET ADMIRAL

## The Story of William F. Halsey

☆ ☆ ☆ ☆ ☆

*by* LAWRENCE A. KEATING

THE WESTMINSTER PRESS
*Philadelphia*

Permission to quote from the following has been granted by the authors' agent, Brandt & Brandt:

*Aircraft Carrier,* by J. Bryan, III (Ballantine Books, Inc.)

"Never a Battle Like Midway," by J. Bryan, III (Curtis Publishing Company)

*Admiral Halsey's Story,* by William F. Halsey and J. Bryan, III (Whittlesey House)

LIBRARY OF CONGRESS CATALOG CARD NO. 65-10580

Published by The Westminster Press®
Philadelphia, Pennsylvania

PRINTED IN THE UNITED STATES OF AMERICA

For

Edythe and Kathryn

# Contents

# List of Maps

[Chapter 1]

# "This Is No Drill!"

THE MESSAGE from Washington warned all United States military forces in the Pacific to be alert against surprise attack.

The scene was Pearl Harbor, Hawaii, principal American stronghold in the Far East. The date was November 27, 1941.

In the headquarters map room of Admiral Husband E. Kimmel, commander of the United States Pacific Fleet, bands of gold braid gleamed on the blue sleeves of four admirals and silver stars shone on the shoulders of two generals of the Army and the Air Force. For more than a year these men had judged war with Japan to be drawing steadily nearer. In spite of diplomatic negotiations continuing in Washington as Prime Minister Tojo's special envoys professed to seek " settlement of mutual problems," they feared that the Empire of the Rising Sun might strike first and declare war later. Japan had done that against Russia in 1904 and against China in 1937.

Stockiest of the admirals present was square-built William Frederick Halsey, Jr. His rank was vice admiral, his signal number 41, which marked him forty-first among the several thousand officers of the United States Navy. Friends called him Bill. Some enlisted men aboard his flagship, the aircraft carrier *Enterprise*, nicknamed him Bull, as fitting his rugged character. No one called him Bull to his face.

Almost six feet tall, Bill Halsey looked shorter. Though he

weighed only 165 pounds, he looked heavier. Among the "scrambled eggs" decorated uniform caps on the rack near the conference room door, Halsey's had to be specially made to fit his large head. He had quick, sharp blue eyes. His jaw was massive, but aides said he smiled more than he scowled. Often, they explained, his scowls were caused by impatiently trying to read without his glasses.

The conferees reviewed their long-formulated plans for best distributing Pearl Harbor's meager fighting units. These comprised ground and air forces under General Walter C. Short, commander of the Hawaiian Department of the Army, and Admiral Kimmel's eighty-six ships, including the several dozen tugs, tankers, supply and repair vessels necessary to maintain a fleet.

The Army, responsible for land defense of the Islands – principally Oahu – was short of antiaircraft weapons and experienced personnel to man them. The Air Force, though counting 231 planes, had only a handful of bombers and P-36 and P-40 fighters ready for combat. The Navy's most desperate shortage was patrol planes and trained crews.

Navy's responsibility was the offshore guarding of Hawaii. To guard it adequately called for a continuous eight-hundred-mile, 360-degree search for hostile craft by patrol planes, scout submarines, and fast surface ships. With the forces at Admiral Kimmel's disposal, such vigilance was not possible.

He lacked enough planes to maintain close scrutiny of even a 60-degree sector. In addition he was required to transfer a dozen flight crews to the United States each month to help train recruits in the fast-expanding Naval Aviation schools. This left him two choices: to keep all his remaining air crews and planes on continuous search, or always to hold some back which would be ready for defense in case of attack. He held some back.

One thing Admiral Kimmel could do and did was maintain his fighting ships in battle readiness. He divided them into

Task Forces 1, 2, and 3 and ordered that only one force was to be in port at a time. This was to avoid the Pacific Fleet's being trapped and annihilated, and to keep up a maximum of scouting at sea.

Twenty months ago, because of gathering war clouds, the Navy Department had flashed the curt order, "Strip." On all ships flammable and splinterable material not required for combat use had been removed: boats, cushions, wooden chests, canvas deck awnings, excess cordage, and paint. Steel splinter shields were placed in position to protect antiaircraft gun crews. Degaussing cables around vessels' hulls under water to neutralize magnetic mines were installed, and listening gear to detect submarines.

Radar was new. Over the past year as ships returned to the Fleet after overhaul at mainland Navy yards they wore "those bedsprings on the foremast," as sailors called the elaborate antennae. Halsey had conducted special sea drills of his Task Force 2 in use of radar until all screen signals and nulls (blind spots) could be quickly and accurately interpreted.

Concerning the overall situation at Pearl Harbor, Admiral Halsey later declared:

> Even an ideal man can't do a job without proper tools, and Kimmel did not have them. The blame falls on the ostrich policy which the United States adopted after World War I. We refused to recognize the existence of predatory nations; therefore they did not exist. On the theory that sweetness and light would prevail and that we would have no further need for the Navy, appropriations were cut and cut again. Enlistments had to be restricted; ships were laid up; few new ships were built.
>
> Providentially, President Roosevelt came into office in time to save our military establishment from complete collapse. He began to restore it at once and although it was perilously—almost fatally—weak when war broke out, he had managed to shore it up enough to survive the first assault.

Half around the world there was likelihood of the United States becoming involved in another war, with Nazi Germany. Most Americans considered Europe close and important to us, but Japan far away and of little importance. The largest part of our fleet was kept in the Atlantic. In the Pacific, Japanese armament outweighed ours in almost every category. In aircraft carriers alone we had three, none with her full operational quota of planes. Japan had nine carriers fully equipped.

The high officers at Pearl Harbor believed that should Japan make any kind of surprise attack, it would be aimed southward, the general direction in Asia in which she was ambitiously expanding. If her target was the Malay Peninsula, as seemed likely, the United States would have more time to prepare. Hawaii, after all, was about four thousand miles from Japan. If Pearl should be struck, doubtless it would be by a large force of submarines synchronized with a shore outbreak of sabotage by the 155,000 Hawaiian residents of Japanese birth.

Today the admirals and generals felt special concern for those tiny dots in the vast Pacific called Midway, Wake, Johnston, and Palmyra. Hundreds of miles from Pearl, these islands formed a far-out picket line expected to receive the first brunt of any attack. Wake and Midway had recently built airfields, still almost empty, which the Army and Navy departments had agreed to stock. Halsey's assignment now was to deliver fighter planes to them from his carrier *Enterprise*.

Discussion turned to whether these planes should be the latest type available or older models.

"They'll probably be our first to meet the enemy. Let's send the best," urged General Short.

Halsey turned to Air Force General Martin. "Aren't your pursuit pilots forbidden to venture more than fifteen miles from shore?"

That was true, the general acknowledged.

"Then they will be too short-range for our purpose. To do this job we need men trained to navigate over water."

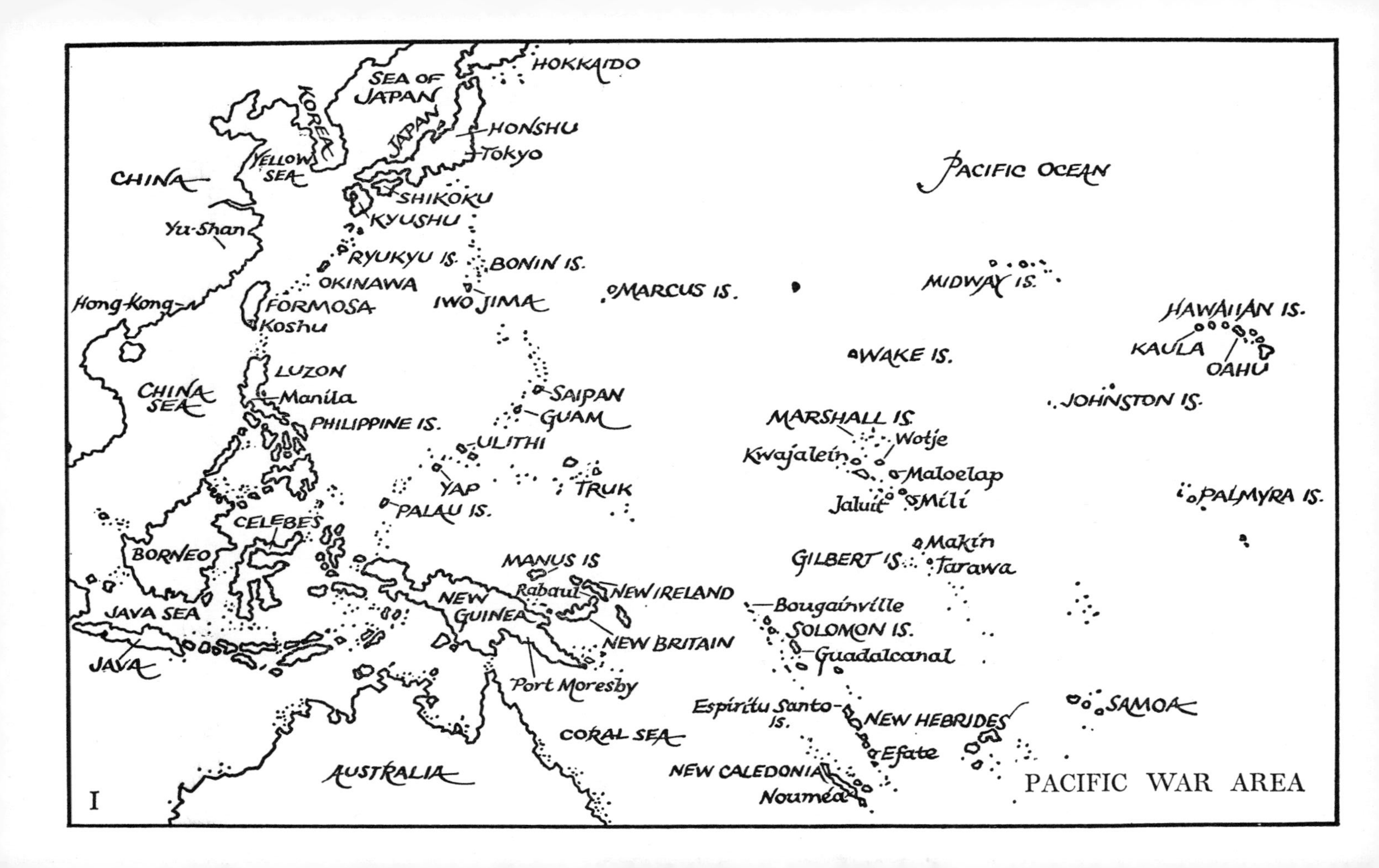


PACIFIC WAR AREA

Agreement was reached to send a dozen of the latest model F4F Marine fighter planes. The conference broke up. After lunch Halsey returned to Kimmel's office and remained with him until six o'clock, talking over the project.

Ready at last to leave Fleet headquarters he asked, " How far do you want me to go? "

Admiral Kimmel's reply was as fine an order, Halsey believed, as a subordinate ever received. " Use your common sense," was all Kimmel said. That gave full authority to deal with any situation as Halsey judged best, with the assurance of complete backing.

Secrecy was imperative lest some local Japanese agent radio Tokyo that Wake and Midway Islands were being armed with planes. Except for those attending the conference, only two officers knew about Halsey's assignment, one of them Major Paul Putnam, commander of Marine Fighter Squadron 211. To get his pilots aboard the *Enterprise* that night without arousing speculation, Putnam announced they were bound for two days of experimental work. The men filed aboard carrying only overnight kits.

Task Force 2 sailed from Pearl at 0700 on November 28.

Taking along his three battleships gave Japanese spies the impression, Halsey hoped, that he was bound for a routine Fleet exercise. Once out of sight of Oahu, however, he divided his squadron. Task Force 2 under Admiral Milo Draemel, comprising the battleships with cruiser and destroyer escorts, proceeded toward the drill grounds for normal work. The ships Halsey retained, now called Task Force 8, comprised the *Enterprise,* known as " the *Big E,*" three heavy cruisers, and nine destroyers. This group stood eastward in pretense of a roundabout course for sortie later with Task Force 2.

Halsey thus divided his strength in order to deliver the Marine planes to Wake as quickly as possible. The battleships' best pace was seventeen knots as against thirty for the *Enterprise* and her cruisers and destroyers. He also reasoned that in the event of meeting the Japanese fleet, Task Force 8's speed would be more protection than the big guns of the ponderous battle-wagons.

Once the two forces were out of signal distance of each other and Pearl Harbor, Halsey requested Captain George Murray of the *Enterprise* to issue Battle Order No. 1. It began:

1. The *Enterprise* is now operating under war conditions.
2. At any time, day or night, we must be ready for instant action.
3. Hostile submarines may be encountered.

A general signal to TF 8 directed that war heads be fitted to torpedoes on all vessels, and planes be armed with live bombs or torpedoes. Sure that no American or Allied shipping was in these waters, Halsey ordered his air patrol pilots to sink any ship sighted and to shoot down any unidentified plane.

Reading this order twice before he could believe it, Operations Officer William Buracker rushed to find Halsey. " Admiral, did you authorize this? "

" I did."

" But, sir, do you realize it can mean war? "

" I am prepared to destroy any snoopers, preferably before they can make radio report of our presence."

Buracker appealed, " But, Admiral! You can't start a private war of your own. Who's going to take the responsibility? "

" I am," Halsey snapped. " If anything gets in my way, we'll shoot first and talk things over afterward."

All task force radios fell silent. During daylight hours the *Big E*'s aircraft maintained continuous antisubmarine patrol. Each morning and evening the ocean over a three-hundred-mile radius was thoroughly searched. Bill Halsey hoped that if Japan meant to make war on the United States, he might be just quick enough to strike first. Not that he expected to meet Japanese warships four thousand miles from their bases, for yesterday's Washington warning again supported the belief that the Japanese would strike southward. But if there should be an encounter in these waters, Halsey assumed it would mean they were en route to a sneak attack on Pearl Harbor.

The sixth day at sea the bristling steel silhouettes of Task Force 8 slowed to half-speed. The *Enterprise*'s helmsman slowly brought her around until her bow nosed into the wind. High on her lopsided-looking deck island, on the admiral's bridge, Halsey leaned on the rail and watched the Marine fliers take off. One by one, planes raced up the flight deck and leaped out over the sea. A moment each faltered in choppy air currents, then steadying, began to climb in slowly widening circles. As the last F4F became airborne, sister planes waiting in the sky swung into flight formation.

Major Putnam waggled his fighter's wings in farewell. The men of Squadron 211 began their two-hundred-mile run to Wake Island . . . and to four miserable years in Japanese prison camps.

Now Task Force 8 came about and picked up speed on the shortest course back to Pearl Harbor. Estimated arrival time, allowing for a rendezvous with tankers to refuel, was 0730 hours December 7. But heavy swells that repeatedly snapped fuel hoses between tankers and pitching destroyers forced several hours' delay. Dawn that historic 7th found the *Big E*'s cutwater still plowing green two hundred miles west of Hawaii.

Halsey ordered eighteen of his planes launched to fly ashore to Ford Island Naval Air Station, part of the Pearl Harbor Complex. A pilot himself and always anxious for safe takeoffs and landings, he again watched operations from his bridge. The last plane gone, he turned indoors and walked among flag plot duty men to his private quarters to shave and dawdle in the bathroom the way he liked to.

A fleet admiral or task force commander takes no part in operating his host ship, but as the guest of its skipper, is furnished space and communications for his functioning. This space is called flag bridge and flag plot.

Flag plot, a room the size of a handball court, gave onto a horseshoe-shaped bridge that provided observation in all directions. Plot and bridge hung on the forward end of the *Big E*'s island eighty feet above her waterline and one level above the pilothouse, which was the ship's nerve center and her captain's command post. On flag bridge, speaking tubes led into flag plot and there were mounts for signalmen's searchlights and telescopes.

Flag plot was the admiral's office. To this center came all battle and fleet information. The room was manned at all hours, but in time of action manned more heavily. Radiomen brought dispatches. Coded messages rasped out of squawk boxes. Red lights flashing meant air plot had just-returned pilots standing by to report what they had seen and accomplished. Signalmen brought in messages taken by blinker or semaphore from other ships. From flag bridge came the piped voices of observers; and Marine orderlies and Intelligence officers came and went. Visible to all, a maze of dials and clock faces on the wall included the compass, the speed log, the dead reckoning tracer, anemometer giving wind velocity and direction, and the plan position indicator, which showed the locations of nearby ships.

The chief quartermaster and duty quartermaster maintained the official flag plot log, entering all decisions made. An officer wearing earphones plotted the positions of airborne planes as reported from the ship's combat information center on another deck. A yeoman typed every word of radioed talk between ships. Behind a curtain, radar men kept twenty-four hour vigil over their scope. With the necessary desks, chairs, plotting boards, files, typewriters, and personnel, the room was crowded and bustling. Bells rang, lights flashed, loudspeakers mumbled. All the information that flowed into flag plot was channeled to a half dozen staff officers and from them to the chief of staff and the admiral.

From this room the task force was led. Here a battle was planned and the battle was fought. During it, all ports and doors were dogged shut so that those at work in flag plot could see and know nothing except what came to them over radio and wires and through tubes.

The admiral's simple but comfortable private quarters were

off flag plot so that asleep or awake he could be in instant touch with the latest happenings. His time at sea was largely passed within this small apartment-size area of bridge, office, and cabin.

Later that morning, in fresh khaki trousers and shirt, tieless, his collar open, Bill Halsey went to the messroom for breakfast.

By tradition, lower ranks in an admiral's mess do not speak unless spoken to save for an occasional, "Please pass the butter." Bill Halsey, however, sought a relaxed atmosphere. He encouraged every staff member to join in whatever was under discussion. Now, as always when he appeared, his aides dropped knives and forks and sprang to their feet. As always, hands on hips, the Old Man exclaimed,

"Sit down, sit down! How often must I tell you?" But twinkling blue eyes offset that beetle-browed scowl.

Later, sipping a second cup of coffee, he listened idly as Lieutenant Douglas Moulton answered the telephone connected with flag plot. "This is Moulton. *What!* Yes. Roger!" He hung up.

The lieutenant's cheeks whitened as he turned. "Admiral! The staff duty officer says he has a message that there's an air raid on Pearl!"

Halsey jumped up. "That must mean they're shooting at our men flying in. Get word off to Kimmel!"

The staff exchanged looks of dismay. Trigger-happy AA gunners ashore, they agreed without speaking, must have failed to recognize American planes. Next moment Lieutenant Commander Dow burst into the messroom and handed Halsey the dispatch from Commander in Chief, Pacific Fleet.

From: CINCPAC
To: All ships present
AIR RAID ON PEARL HARBOR X THIS IS NO DRILL

[Chapter 2]

# Sneak Attack

MINUTES LATER came two verifications. Hostilities with Japan had commenced with the violent assault still continuing on Pearl Harbor.

The beat of Task Force 8 engines increased to top speed. Pacing flag bridge, Halsey awaited orders from Admiral Kimmel. Because of the Japanese air raid, probably Halsey would not be wanted at Pearl and in any case could not arrive there for another seven hours. What he hoped was to learn the whereabouts of the enemy striking force. Little more than half of the *Big E*'s plane complement remained aboard, a meager force to pit against scores of fighters on the several carriers he knew must be taking part in the raid; nevertheless Bill Halsey itched to find and attack Japanese ships.

His patrol planes searching the summer skies reported no sign of the enemy. At 0921 Kimmel's message came.

From: CINCPAC
To: Task Forces 3–8–12
RENDEZVOUS AS CTF 8 DIRECTS X FURTHER INSTRUCTIONS WHEN ENEMY LOCATED

Task Force 3, commanded by Admiral Wilson Brown, was also at sea, divided in much the same way Halsey had split his own squadron. Its subsidiary, known as 12, should be on its way back from ferrying Marine planes to Midway Island. The remainder of Brown's Number 3, a heavy cruiser and a few destroyers, was far off in the vicinity of Johnston Island. In addition, all ships at Pearl able to get under way and escape were ordered to join Halsey.

Thus he was given operational command of all our combat ships at sea. Admiral Kimmel was striving to assemble a battle force to find and engage the attacking Japanese fleet.

It would be hours before the nearest American vessels could close with Halsey and might be two or three days for the farthest. Meanwhile the *Enterprise* and her escorts cruised off Kaula Rock a hundred fifty miles west of Pearl. Suddenly an old four-stack destroyer came boiling over the eastern horizon. She would have sped past without contact, but Halsey signaled, "Where are you headed?"

"Don't know. Ordered to steam west top speed."

"Join us," Halsey requested and quoted his authority. He turned, grinning to an aide. "At that pace, if her fuel held out, she'd eventually have piled up on the China coast."

False reports began to pour in on the flagship. Some may have originated with the Japanese fleet for the purpose of causing confusion, others from espionage centers in the Hawaiian Islands. One, later proved true, said a U.S. patrol plane had sunk a submarine off the channel entrance to Pearl. Most were alarming but not true, the mistakes of inexperienced scout plane pilots and young seamen who tended to see in distant clouds enemy planes that were not there and to mistake playing porpoises for attacking submarines.

Which reports were reliable? Each one had to be presumed so until disproved. This cost time and fuel as capital ships veered away at full power from reported danger while destroyers raced here and there dropping depth charges. When the *Benham,* trailing the *Big E,* disappeared in the trough of a wave a young officer on the bridge cried, "She's sinking! There she goes!"

Halsey, watching through glasses, saw the destroyer bob

safely over the next crest. " If you ever make another report like that, sir," he exploded, " I'll throw you over the side! "

Lookout nervousness seemed to increase. At last Halsey radioed a scolding to his whole force that ended, " We are wasting too many depth charges on fish."

Late in the afternoon Admiral Draemel messaged that he feared Admiral Pye's battleships caught in Pearl Harbor had been incapacitated. However, so far there was no authoritative report of the damage inflicted by the Japanese.

A new dispatch located an enemy fleet to the southwest. Immediately the *Enterprise* threw more planes into the air. Forming a scouting line of all other Task Force 2 ships, Halsey sent them to search with orders to open fire on contact. No contact was made. Another report located an enemy aircraft carrier south of Pearl, and spoiling for the fight that kept eluding him, Halsey launched his last twenty-one planes of Torpedo Squadron 6 to attack, along with six smoke planes and six fighters.

There was no carrier. The planes, still armed with dangerous live torpedoes, had great difficulty returning to the bouncing deck of the *Big E*. The fighters flew off to Pearl. There, despite radio notice of their coming, the still jittery AA gunners shot down four – as that morning five of the eighteen *Enterprise* planes had been shot down.

" When you've been watching your ships bombed and your buddies killed," growled one gunner, " no plane looks friendly."

Cruising all night, the *Enterprise* and her sister ships awaited dependable scouting information. If the enemy were located, Halsey realized, the odds in a pitched battle were steadily mounting against him. He had only cruisers to oppose the sixteen- and possibly eighteen-inch rifles of battleships. He had only a handful of planes left for both attack and defense. Equally worrysome was fuel. The nightmare of every commander is to have his ship dead in the water because fuel is exhausted. Halsey's cruisers were down to 30 percent and the tanks of his destroyers averaged only 20 percent.

Next day came more bad guesses and mirages. A scout plane reported making an unopposed attack on a Japanese carrier near Johnston Island. Soon it identified the "carrier" as our heavy cruiser *Portland.* The truth was, American forces both at Pearl and at sea were still in shock from the Japanese raid.

It was near sundown December 8 when Task Force 2, in a line of ships, moved slowly up the channel into Pearl Harbor. On his bridge Bill Halsey gripped the rail, white-faced and speechless. The havoc he saw in ship after ship was almost too much to believe. There, for one, lay the veteran battlewagon *Utah,* sunk. Had it not been for bad weather delaying Task Force 8's refueling at sea the *Enterprise* would have occupied that very anchorage.

Pearl Harbor inlet, with its spacious bay and extensions reaching out like tree branches, is on the south shore of Oahu. Ford Island in the harbor was the Naval Air Station. Across the water the Navy Yard with its labyrinth of drydocks, machine shops, arsenals, warehouses, and tank farms stood ready to repair, supply, and fuel all units of the Fleet from admirals' barges to battleships.

Chief concentration of the Army was at Schofield Barracks inland. Airfields dotting Oahu were Hickam, Bellows, Wheeler, Ewa, and Kaneohe, in addition to Ford Island.

At a secret meeting the previous February in Tokyo, Admiral Isoroku Yamamoto, commander of the Japanese Combined Fleet, had proposed a devastating raid on Pearl Harbor. "If we are to have war with America," he warned a carefully chosen group of high officers, "we can have no hope of victory until their Pacific Fleet is destroyed."

How to smash that Fleet at one blow? It was known that American strategists believed an attack, if one ever came, would be by submarine, aided by shore sabotage. Admiral Yamamoto, however, saw that such an attack must fall short of the shattering blow Japan needed.

He knew that in the American Navy, as in his own, the modern battleship was still considered by most flag officers to be the world's mightiest weapon. Aircraft were looked upon as operational tools; carriers, as a sort of courtesy, were called "the eyes of the Fleet." Enthusiasts for capital ships challenged, "When has a first-class battlewagon ever been sunk by planes?" To date, none ever had been. But Yamamoto, like a few other imaginative tacticians – Bill Halsey among them – saw the dawn of a new day in naval warfare. He appreciated the worth of aircraft carriers' high speed, the tremendous mobile striking power of planes and their swift coverage of hundreds of miles of open ocean.

He proposed to destroy the United States Pacific Fleet from aircraft carriers, six of them, standing well to sea. They would reach the shore with the largest flight of planes ever seen. At once began the immense amount of planning necessary to carry out this operation.

In Pearl Harbor on any given day it was normal to count thirty or more destroyers, a dozen cruisers, and three to six battleships. Additionally, on strike day, Yamamoto hoped, one or more of our carriers would be in port. It was unusual that on December 7 eight battleships were at Pearl, though no carriers. Six of the battleships were in Admiral Pye's task force and it was not his turn at sea. Of the others, the *Pennsylvania* and *Arizona* were undergoing repairs and the old *Utah* now was used as a gunnery target.

The very anchorages off Ford Island of our capital ships favored the enemy. Lying in pairs were the *Maryland* and *Oklahoma;* the *Tennessee* and *West Virginia;* the *Arizona* and repair ship *Vestal.* Ahead of these pairs lay the *Nevada* and behind them the *California.* The *Utah* was off the other side of the island.

That Sunday morning was warm, sunny, and peaceful. At 0730 most ship commanders and staff officers still were ashore at their homes. Aboard the vessels few men were on duty. Some off duty were at breakfast, others shaving and dressing, expecting to leave soon by launch to attend church services. A few planned picnics or to go fishing. On the *Nevada*'s main deck her band, with the usual joking and small talk, began to assemble to play Morning Colors at eight o'clock. On the *Maryland* an off-duty seaman climbed to a machine-gun nest where he would not be disturbed while he addressed Christmas cards to his friends in the States.

Admiral Chuichi Nagumo, commanding the Japanese striking force, had been at sea nearly a month. Because peace negotiations continued in Washington, the admiral had to cruise aimlessly, waiting for the final order to attack. In Tokyo on December 1 the Imperial Council decided on war and the next day – diplomatic overtures with America still going on – Admiral Yamamoto radioed to Nagumo: "Climb Mount Nikata." It was code for: "Proceed with the attack."

With all combat ships refueled, Nagumo ordered his eight tankers to start homeward. His attack force comprised twenty ships: six aircraft carriers, two battleships, three cruisers, nine destroyers, and twenty-seven submarines. For the first time, five two-man submarines were to be used.

On the carriers three hundred fifty-three torpedo planes, dive bombers, and high-level bombers were available for the two-wave assault. Thirty-nine other planes were retained for air patrol around the striking force and for reserve. From Nagumo's fleet, standing a hundred seventy-five miles at sea, the first wave of a hundred eighty-three planes took off at 0600. The second, numbering a hundred seventy, would follow an hour and a quarter later.

On Oahu at an Army radar station a rookie operator stayed on to practice after his duty ended. He plotted a large number of approaching planes more than a hundred miles to the north. He rechecked, then excitedly telephoned his report. An officer, remembering that a dozen unarmed B-17's were expected in from the States, soothed him with, "Don't worry about it."

The Japanese arrived at 0755 hours. Over the next fifteen minutes hundreds of servicemen found it hard to believe that, as one said, " This was for keeps."

A colonel at Hickam Field, watching a line of fighter aircraft sweep nearer, remarked to a lieutenant, " Very realistic. But why so early on Sunday? "

When a bomb exploded near the cruiser *Honolulu,* one Marine bet another a dollar it was the Army staging a mock surprise attack on the Navy, using dummy torpedoes.

On the *California* the General Quarters alarm made a fireman deep in her engine room complain, " What a time to be holdin' a drill! "

A sergeant of the 27th Infantry refused to unlock a magazine of automatic rifle ammunition " to repel the invasion " because he had no order from his adjutant, who was nowhere around.

With a tremendous explosion a torpedo crippled the cruiser *Helena.* General Quarters sounded. In her engine room one of the men thought this must be some officer's bright idea for getting the crew to attend church.

At Kaneohe airfield an ensign raged, " Some fool Army pilot just strafed our quarters! "

Six low-flying torpedo planes machine-gunned a launch chugging toward shore. Its passengers decided those red circles painted on the planes must indicate some new squadron from the States. When one sailor slumped groaning with a bullet in his stomach, the others changed their minds.

The truth dawned very slowly all over Pearl Harbor that those scores of planes roaring overhead were not American. They were not flying for practice. The bombs they were dropping were intended to kill.

Two aerial torpedoes blasted the *Utah.* They caused two sickening lurches and raised blinding columns of smoke, dirt, and water. Slowly the great ship rolled over on her side, trapping many crewmen inside her hull.

A dropped torpedo skimmed across Ford Island, disappeared

in the water, and passed under the mine layer *Oglala*. It hit the *Helena* next to her and exploded in the engine room. The *Helena* sank. The concussion opened the *Oglala*'s seams and she also sank.

Two torpedoes penetrated the *California* below her waterline. While she settled, oil from ruptured fuel tanks rapidly spread on the water around her. It caught fire. Diving into this inferno, many of her crew were lost; others swam to safety. The *West Virginia*, though hit six times, stayed upright, some of her AA guns still barking while slowly she went down. The *Arizona*, receiving four heavy bombs and with a torpedo straight down her smokestack, was a complete wreck. Of her crew eleven hundred and two were trapped inside her hull and perished. The *Nevada*, although hit, managed in lumbering fashion to get under way. She soon ran aground. The *Oklahoma*, wounded and torn by five torpedoes, tiredly turned on her side.

Smaller craft were crippled, set afire, or sunk. With an explosion like a warehouse of fireworks going off, the destroyer *Shaw* blew completely apart. Side by side in their slip the *Cassin* and *Downes* were wrecked. On the badly damaged cruiser *Raleigh*, her commander and crew fought valiantly to keep her afloat by pumps and by stuffing mattresses into gaping holes in her hull. Docks, a few warehouses, and oil tanks were set afire and the sun was blacked out by a score of mile-high columns of thick, oily smoke.

Few ships in the harbor could get into motion because few had steam up. To develop sufficient boiler pressure took a battleship two and a half hours. It took a cruiser two hours, a destroyer one hour. Before the Japanese last aerial strike ended at 0945 hours a few destroyers did manage to get under way and went racing out the channel looking for enemy ships. The whereabouts of Admiral Nagumo's striking force remained unknown.

On Oahu airfields, planes were close-parked in rows and for months had been guarded against much-feared sabotage — of which there was none. This method of parking offered rich targets to strafing Japanese pilots. They demolished or set fire to row after row. Then they came again to wreck any planes missed.

The attackers' complete surprise made effective defense slow to organize. However, amid difficulties fast worsening, the men of the Army and Navy fought back with every weapon they could get hold of from .45 caliber automatics to antiaircraft guns. Scrappy morale remained high and in two hours scores of heroes were born. And scores died.

American casualties were twenty-three hundred forty-three men killed, twelve hundred seventy-two wounded, and nine hundred sixty missing. Eighteen ships were sunk or seriously damaged. At the airfields a hundred seventy-seven planes were destroyed on the ground and a hundred fifty-nine others were damaged.

Japanese losses were forty-eight planes, one submarine, and the five midget two-man submarines. Personnel losses were about one hundred.

The Pearl Harbor raid was a smashing victory for Japan. For the United States it was a staggering defeat.

[Chapter 3]

# Fighting Back

EAGER to battle Japanese and half expecting a follow-up aerial strike, after only one night in port, the *Enterprise* and her escorts next morning put to sea. She began to patrol northward to hunt out the enemy and, in particular, Japanese submarines that were believed to be en route to raid shipping along the American west coast. Already an unidentified aircraft carrier was reported sighted off California. Halsey's search planes found no submarines, and in a few days California decided that the " carrier " was a lumber-loaded merchantman.

Although Navy officers believed Admiral Kimmel had done all any man could have, at his own request he was relieved as commander in chief of the Pacific Fleet. Admiral Pye was his temporary successor. On the mainland a nationwide wail of dismay prompted President Roosevelt to appoint a commission to investigate the Pearl Harbor disaster. After months of deliberation the Roberts Commission in effect blamed our lack of preparedness. This was no news to top Pacific commanders. But public indignation demanded scapegoats, and, helpless to defend themselves in the face of the national anger, Admiral Kimmel and General Short saw the shadows fall on their careers.

Meanwhile, for Bill Halsey there followed other short searches for the enemy, but the ocean was vast and intelligence scant. Tiny Guam, thirty-three hundred miles away, had already fallen to the Japanese. Wake, hardly more than a large atoll, was under attack. For its relief, one task force was hurried to bomb Japanese-held Wotje to divert attention; Halsey's Task Force 8 sailed to cover the northern flank around Midway; and Task Force 14, led by the carrier *Saratoga,* rushed men and planes to reinforce Wake.

When the *Saratoga* reached launching distance with fighter planes warming their engines on her deck, an order, never explained, came for her to turn away from the area. Instead, the aircraft tender *Tangier,* much smaller and lacking air cover, was to go in. Already the enemy were landing and Wake radio warned " situation in doubt." The *Sara*'s plane crews, forbidden to help their comrades ashore, sat down on her deck and wept in frustration. Two days later Wake's defenders were overwhelmed.

For Task Force 8, pursuit, at an expensive twenty-five knots, of enemy concentrations that were not there, plus guarding convoys of men, planes, and munitions arriving from the States, filled the next two weeks. Halsey returned to Pearl early in January of 1942. In Washington the new CINCUS (Commander in Chief, United States Fleet) was Admiral Ernest King. Shortly, by air, he sent Admiral Chester Nimitz to Hawaii as the new CINCPAC. Bill Halsey knew both men and their capabilities well. Handed the news in his flag plot, he pounded a jubilant fist on his desk.

" Now this diddling and hysteria will stop. You'll see things begin to happen! "

Admiral Nimitz summoned him to conference at Pearl Harbor. White-haired and of medium build, Nimitz habitually wore a gentle expression and spoke in a soft voice. Halsey, however, declared he was " iron underneath." Though longtime friends, they wasted not a minute on pleasantries, but plunged at once into planning.

On his wall map Nimitz indicated the British-owned Gilbert Islands forty-five hundred miles southwest of Pearl. " The Japs have just occupied these. Probably their next jump will be another thirteen hundred miles to Samoa."

His pointer swung far westward to the Philippines. "They attacked Manila the day after they raided Pearl. Fighting still goes on, but the enemy can pour in a couple of hundred thousand troops and all the planes they can use. Our skimpy Asiatic Fleet and General MacArthur's troops can't hold out. And we can't send much help. I give MacArthur a couple of months."

He paused. "Once the Japs have solid control of the Philippines and of the Gilberts and of Samoa nearer us, they will go on to try to block our routes to New Zealand and Australia."

The significance of this was well known to Bill Halsey. Closing off New Zealand and Australia with their contributions of fighting men and vast quantities of wool and meat could mean a staggering blow. Japanese supremacy in the central, south, and southwest Pacific would not only jeopardize the struggle in this hemisphere but thousands of miles away weaken the American and British war in the Atlantic and Europe against Hitler's Nazi Germany.

Nimitz continued, "But we're just not giving the enemy their way. We must begin hitting them, and hard. So far we lack amphibious strength to grab Jap territory or to win back our own." His keen eyes held Halsey's. "Which means — "

"Fast carrier attacks? Hit and run?"

"Exactly. We've got to damage them. Slow down their advance.

"Here is the plan," he went on. "We're bringing out Marines to reinforce Samoa. They're on their way from San Diego this minute in Frank Fletcher's Task Force 17. Fletcher is on the *Yorktown*, so we gain another carrier. I want you to rendezvous with 17. Guard Fletcher while he lands those Marines. Then lead 17 and your 8 against the Marshall group and also the Gilberts."

In the planning of such a strike, the lack of information about the Marshall Islands lying north of the Gilberts posed a worry.

They had been mandated to Japan after World War I with the proviso that they were never to be fortified. Ever since, the Japanese had permitted no foreigner ashore, so it was obvious they had violated their pledge and probably built airfields and submarine bases.

Over several hours the two admirals worked out details of the venture. Next day after another short meeting Nimitz walked with Halsey to the dock and his waiting admiral's barge. " All sorts of good luck to you, Bill! "

Life aboard combat ships was now more grim and exacting than before the onset of hostilities. Where before the public address bugle call for Air Alert or the more urgent clang of General Quarters throughout the ship meant an unexpected drill, now it meant a potential battle. Wherever a man off duty might be, whether at mess or writing letters or asleep, the sounding of GQ propelled him to instant motion toward his battle station. Often it was in some distant or lofty part of the ship. A new arrival aboard was careful to use his first free moments to explore his best route up ladders, along dark passageways, across decks, and up more ladders. The shortest route was not always fastest because on a big ship hundreds of men simultaneously boiled through her decks, rushing in all directions to their stations.

The allowance was two minutes to get from wherever you were to where you were wanted. A lieutenant sharing a tiny inside room below the hangar deck on the *Enterprise*, if caught asleep, had to don his clothes in seconds. Before dozing off, he would by habit have arranged them within arm's length. Bursting out of his door, he knew how many steps he must take to the foot of the hangar deck ladder because if the lights should be out, this knowledge would save bruised shins. He knew how many rungs on the ladder, then the distance across the hangar deck to a steel door that opened onto a spiral stairway. If his duty post was on flag bridge, he must sprint across flight deck, dodging planes and men, to the island, then upward inside it.

" I am the only swab in this man's Navy," boasted one bosun's mate on the *Big E,* " who can pull on his socks runnin' at full gallop! "

To delay belowdecks not only meant being absent from one's post but also getting locked away for the emergency. For as the two-minute warning lapsed, all over the ship steel doors ground and squeaked closed. They were centrally controlled to secure the ship against the spread of fire or flooding. Once the doors blocked your way, you were imprisoned. When the big guns' pounding shattered light bulbs and you pictured torpedoes streaking toward the hull beside which you stood, it was pleasanter not to be shut away in the dark.

In addition to emergency use, General Quarters was stood regularly in combat zones an hour before dawn and an hour after dark, the likeliest times for attack. GQ was sounded when a task force trailed out of Pearl Harbor channel or returned to it from the sea. It sounded so often unexpectedly that when at mess a man buttered a slice of toast, he had no assurance that he would ever get to eat it before the panicky clanging of General Quarters.

Rather than the good luck Nimitz had wished Halsey, bad luck seemed to dog his way to rendezvous with Task Force 17. Word came that the *Saratoga* had been torpedoed. She was steaming back to the States, where repairs would consume several months. Thus instead of the *Yorktown* adding to our Pacific carrier strength, it remained at three with the *Enterprise* and *Lexington.* Next, a scout plane pilot endangered Halsey's entire expedition by breaking radio silence to report engine trouble. A seaman on the cruiser *Salt Lake City* died in a turret accident; and an incoming *Enterprise* plane crashed on her deck, killing a machinist's mate.

Ill luck had not finished. One of the *Big E*'s torpedo planes failed to return. Task Force 8 dared not pause for a search. For thirty-four days the three-man plane crew, with little food and water, drifted seven hundred fifty miles in a rubber raft under the broiling tropical sun, but at last reached an island called

Pukapuka. When, months later, the men rejoined Halsey and he pinned decorations on them, he asked Harold Dixon, " Are you still speaking to me after the way I sailed off and left you? "

" Yes, sir," Dixon said. " We knew you had to do it."

The jinx of this trip continued when a plane taking off crashed in the water with two casualties. Another plane scored a direct hit on an enemy submarine, but its torpedo failed to explode. During a blinding rain the destroyers *Fanning* and *Gridley* smashed into each other with such damage to their bows that they had to crawl at slow speed back to Pearl. A schooner encountered failed to give the correct recognition signal to cruiser *Northampton's* scout plane, which promptly bombed and strafed her. She turned out to be British, hunting a plane lost from the *Salt Lake City*.

At least good luck attended the meeting at sea with Task Force 17 and the landing of Marines on Samoa. The plan next called for Admiral Fletcher to bombard Makin in the northern Gilberts and Jaluit and Mili in the southern Marshalls while Halsey struck at other islands. When a reconnaissance submarine reported to him that the entire Marshalls were only light-defended, Halsey faced a hard decision. Should he alter plans to make a bold strike at Kwajalein, the enemy's most strategic island in this area?



The islands, he knew, were ringed by dangerous coral reefs. The only available navigation charts, twenty years old, were believed inaccurate. Too, to get at Kwajalein he would have to risk the *Big E* almost within pistol range when he passed heavily armed Wotje. To risk one of our three precious carriers was a grave responsibility. Yet Kwajalein offered a rich target concentration of enemy shipping and planes.

" If we pull it off, we'll be heroes," Halsey mused. " If we fail we may be court-martialed." He took another turn up and down the bridge. " All right. We'll hit Kwajalein."

He divided Task Force 8 into three groups, two to undertake diversionary strikes at Wotje and Maloelap Islands with heavy bombardment. The *Enterprise,* with destroyers *Ralph Talbot, Blue,* and *McCall,* would concentrate on Kwajalein.

First, refueling of all ships. The *Big E*'s turn at the tanker marked the first time so heavy a ship was refueled in darkness in the open sea. The several-hour operation set up its own tension lest the weather suddenly change or the enemy interrupt. The carrier's thirst was for fifty-two thousand barrels to keep her six-inch fuel pipes gushing day and night like fire hoses into the infernos under her boilers.

Next afternoon as she proceeded, radar blips indicated a Japanese patrol plane. When it turned back, obviously failing to see the warships, Halsey, beaming, summoned his Japanese-language officer.

"Translate this: 'From the American admiral to the Japanese admiral. Thanks to your patrol plane for failing to sight my force.' Tomorrow have our planes drop a few hundred copies of that," Halsey said with a grin. "Maybe it will cause some Nip officer to commit hara-kiri."

Separating, the blacked-out task groups slid through the next night toward their various positions. With operation of his plan now up to the ship commanders, Halsey retired to his cabin so *Big E* crewmen would not see his nervousness. This was his first battle action. He tossed in his bunk, unable to sleep. He tried to divert his thoughts by reading mystery stories. He drank numerous cups of coffee. But his mind still was racing with doubts. At last he gave in to the tension and stalked out to flag plot. The *Big E* was boldly cutting the water at twenty-five knots as if no Japanese were within a hundred miles and there were not the slightest danger of mines.

Others shared the admiral's taut nerves. The staff duty officer rushed in from the bridge. "Sir, we're closing with shore! I just felt sand blow on my face."

"Shore?" Halsey ejaculated. "Shore should be a dozen miles away." Were they, he wondered, about to pile up? "Go back, quick. Investigate!"

The officer did. He returned looking sheepish. "A man on the range-finder platform had a cup of coffee. When he poured sugar into it, some blew my way."

It was bright moonlight when *Enterprise* engines whined lower and she swung her bow into the wind. Nine torpedo bombers raced up her deck and away, each carrying three five-hundred-pound bombs. Thirty-seven dive bombers followed and headed for nearby Roi. Six fighters climbed aloft for air cover.

The moon slid under dark clouds. Heavy mist formed over the sea. In the sky each flier held the beams of his flashlight on a photostat copy of the twenty-year-old chart, searching it for his assigned target. The delay gave the Japanese on Roi time to man AA guns that ringed their airfields and they came snarling alive. Zero fighter planes, faster than ours, rose to challenge the invaders.

"Bandits at twelve o'clock!" Lieutenant Commander Hopping notified his fellow pilots over voice radio. "Best bet is to make your run very low. Hit, then get out of there fast."

Hopping peeled off. With his squadron trailing, he began a power dive at his target. Tracer bullets bit at his wings. Deadly cottonlike AA puffs probed the air around him. Two-engine Japanese bombers, called Bettys, lined up on an airstrip below, rapidly enlarged in his bombsight. Hopping let go his load, the first American bombs to drop on Japanese territory. His lightened plane lifted as if in a strong updraft. Then AA found him and set his plane afire. Like a flaming corkscrew, it spiraled nose-first into the ground.

A few miles away the Kwajalein target proved more profitable. AA was heavy, but there was no fighter plane defense. "It's the jackpot!" the strike leader yelled on radio. "Send more planes. We've got to collect!" Targets in harbor were a light cruiser, two large merchant ships, five submarines, several tankers, and many smaller vessels, besides shore installations. Halsey ordered eighteen planes rerouted from Roi to

Kwajalein and nine more carrying torpedoes launched from the *Big E.*

"He's my pigeon. Keep off!" deck listeners heard from aloft.

"Billy, that's showing the Nips!"

"That sub is still afloat. Better smash her again."

The low-level attack caused some Japanese guns to fire on their own ships and on shore batteries. All *Big E* planes returned safely aboard. The damage estimate was two submarines sunk, six more ships sunk or damaged, two four-engine seaplanes destroyed, and a large shore compound smashed by two direct hits.

Flight sweeps at other islands were synchronized with bombardments by the heavy guns of other task force ships. A Japanese plane planted a bomb on the cruiser *Chester*'s well deck, killing eight men. For nine hours the *Enterprise* had to maneuver up and down within a few square miles while her planes continued to strafe ships and airfields, returned aboard to fuel and rearm, and sped off again. When at last the *Big E* was pulling away, five Bettys suddenly attacked out of the overcast.

Twenty-four AA's and sixteen machine guns on the carrier opened fire. Doggedly the enemy fliers came on. Fifteen bombs fell into the water, one close enough to kill a man in the port after-gun gallery, penetrate the ship's side, and start a gasoline fire. One Betty, with both engines aflame, came screaming down with the evident goal of a crash into planes parked on the flight deck.

Aviation Mechanic Bruno Gaida ran to jump into the rear parked plane. He opened fire with its machine gun. Trying to elude the enemy flier, the *Enterprise* heeled to starboard. The Betty skimmed her deck so close that it knocked the tail off the plane from which Gaida was firing. Then it plunged over the side – the first *kamikaze,* or Japanese suicide plane, of the war.

During this furious action, Bill Halsey said later, he dropped flat on the bridge so quickly that his aides " left footprints on my back." His staff smiled at this. They knew he had simmered with nerves before the shooting started but once in battle was " like icewater."

The *Enterprise* and her destroyers fled at thirty knots with the Japanese, organized now, giving chase in the air. Because our Wildcat fighters were slower, they had to outmaneuver the Bettys and one pilot who did was Lieutenant Commander McClusky. Unseen from the carrier but heard on earphones, McClusky urged a comrade, " Out of my way, Jack. Let me blow that Oriental out of the sky! " Sure enough, fragments of a Betty came raining down on the flight deck.

Pursuit continued as the carrier's boiling wake made a clear moonlit trail. Fighter pilots were not then trained in night takeoffs and landings, so the safety of the *Enterprise* depended on AA gunnery and Captain Murray's twisting, turning navigation. At last rain clouds formed a protective blanket and the *Big E* slipped away.

While Halsey had been battering the bases on the Marshalls, Admiral Fletcher's Task Force 17 had pitched high-explosive shells at Jaluit and Mili, in the southern Marshalls, and Makin in the Gilberts. Bad weather cut short these operations, but some damage was done and for the first time the Japanese had been thrown on the defensive.

At Pearl Harbor on February 5, Task Force 8 crept up the channel. Her crews rubbed their eyes in wonder. Docks and beaches were thronged with blue- and khaki-uniformed welcomers. Ships in harbor blasted their sirens, autos ashore their horns. Troops at Hickam Field and Hospital Point patients on crutches and in wheelchairs were assembled and cheering. A beaming Admiral Nimitz did not wait for the *Big E*'s boarding stairs to be lowered; he came overside in a bosun's chair and rushed to pump Halsey's hand.

" You pulled it off, Bill! "

In the States, news of the Kwajalein strike lifted the nation's morale. Here was proof that although hurt, America could still fight back.

This first blow at Japanese power succeeded because Bill Halsey dared to do the unexpected. Naval strategists always had recommended keeping aircraft carriers safely behind the heavy guns of battleships and cruisers, but he had matched the *Big E*'s planes with shore-based strength and won. His exploit altered battle tactics. It also brought Distinguished Service Medals to Bill Halsey and to his chief of staff, Miles Browning.

[Chapter 4]

# Fliers from Shangri-La

CHECKING over the orders for his next mission, a strike at Wake Island, Bill Halsey was dismayed. "Look at this." He showed Captain Browning. "They've named us Task Force 13, departing Pearl on the thirteenth. What's more, that is a Friday. Are they trying to put a hex on us?"

"Those thirteens would have our crews jittery," Browning agreed.

"Well, you go and have a talk with Admiral Nimitz's staff. Make them assign us some luckier numbers."

Yielding to sailormen's universal superstitions about thirteen and Friday, the task force was redesignated 16 and its sailing date changed. On Saturday, February the fourteenth, at the *Big E*'s signal a destroyer in the bay picked up her hook and began to glide down the channel. Another followed. Another. The heavy cruiser *Salt Lake City* began to move. The *Northampton* swung into her wake. The *Enterprise* was next, trailed by the tanker *Sabine*. Three destroyers in Indian file brought up the rear.

The ships were now wildly camouflaged to make recognition at sea more difficult. As the grim parade neared the mouth of the channel, General Quarters alarms brought every man to his battle station. There was always the possibility of enemy submarines lying in wait off the harbor entrance. The underwater torpedo nets swung wide and TF 16 was on its way.

Once at sea Halsey divided his armament into task groups 16.7 and 16.8. The two heavy cruisers with two destroyers were to approach Wake from the west and ten days hence at 0530 hours were to be fifteen miles offshore in position to deliver heavy bombardment. Simultaneously, planes from the *Enterprise* a hundred miles away would arrive over Wake to strafe Japanese installations. For the first time in Navy history aerial photographs taken by Marine fliers helped to plan the division of targets.

On the appointed day, February 24, wind and rain delayed launching the *Big E*'s planes. Radio silence prevented explaining this to the cruisers. Miles away they waited, not even catapulting their scout planes lest the flash of propulsion charges be noticed ashore. The Japanese spied the cruisers anyway and surprise was lost. Enemy seaplanes beginning to bomb 16.7 were driven off by arriving fighters from the *Enterprise*.

The strafing and bombardment destroyed half a dozen planes, hangars, and damaged shore batteries and fuel and ammunition dumps. Task force losses were one plane to AA and two to bad weather. The raid had no great military value, but it taught the United States the need to strengthen carrier flight squadrons and to furnish plane gunners with incendiary ammunition.

As the *Enterprise* stood away, Halsey was handed a dispatch.

From: CINCPAC
To: CTF 16

DESIRABLE TO STRIKE MARCUS IF YOU THINK IT FEASIBLE

He called his staff into conference. "Marcus Island, Admiral?" An aide studied the chart. "That's awfully near Tokyo, only a thousand miles."

"We don't know about defenses on Marcus," another pointed out. "We do know Iwo Jima is within easy flight and it's a powerhouse."

Halsey pondered. "What about fuel? Could we make it there and back?"

Engineers studied the daily fuel report of each task force ship together with the *Sabine*'s report of her supply. "Sir, we can't refuel in this weather. It may last another two or three days. If we can begin the operation no later than March first, we'll have enough."

"Then we'll go," Halsey decided.

Steaming at economical speed, TF 16 awaited better weather. When the skies cleared, heavy seas still made refueling difficult and slow. At last it was accomplished a day before the deadline, but in this sea, Halsey announced, his destroyers were too light for a prolonged effort at high speed. They stayed behind with the *Sabine* while the *Enterprise, Salt Lake City,* and *Northampton* started their run to Marcus Island.

One hundred and twenty-five miles from it, thirty-two bombers and six fighter planes were launched. Guided by radar, they sped in for attack that took the Japanese unaware. Just as the Wake radio began to scream warning, a direct hit knocked it off the air. Soon a Rising Sun plane came up from Iwo Jima to learn what this disturbance was about. The alert it flashed caused a hasty blackout in far-off Tokyo.

One American bomber was shot down by AA. Ashore, a fuel tank was set afire and airfield buildings were destroyed. There was not much else of value on Marcus to damage, but as Halsey reported, "Hitting the enemy that close to home should show the Japs they are in a real fight."

His return to Pearl Harbor on the tenth of March found Bill Halsey worn and tired. Since the first day of the war he had been in constant motion. Much of the time he had been at sea bearing responsibility for thousands of men's lives, millions of dollars' worth of equipment, and our national security. Nights with little sleep and endless tense hours on the bridge with the salt scud in his face had grooved deep lines. He was plagued by a nagging cough, his skin erupting with eczema probably worsened by overstrained nerves.

But in Admiral Nimitz's office the mention of his next assignment brought his heavy jaw forward, his eyes glinting with interest. Halsey straightened in his chair and his harassed look fell away.

Fleet Admiral King in Washington disliked his CINCUS designation as sounding like " sink us," so had changed it to COMINCH, commander in chief. Representing COMINCH, Admiral Duncan arrived at Pearl to propose an action that made his listeners catch their breath.

" By hitting Marcus Island, Bill," he told Halsey, " you practically rapped on Emperor Hirohito's front door. Got away with it too. Could you do that again? "

" I could try. Maybe this time I can break the door down."

" In your opinion, could Army bombers take off from a carrier's flight deck? "

Halsey frowned his surprise. " I doubt it. Still, that's an interesting thought." He grinned. " Do you mean the Army wants to try? Maybe to bomb Tokyo? "

" Right. Militarily we aren't sure how valuable such a strike would be. But until we get enough strength in this ocean to mount big offensive operations, we've just got to peck away with what we have."

" Such a raid," Nimitz suggested, " will give every American a lift. It should give every Jap a beautiful headache."

" Also," Duncan said, " this job involves the Air Force and Navy working together. You've often said, Bill, that we need to cut out rivalry between the services if we're going to win."

Rising, Halsey looked closer at the wall map of the western Pacific. " What type of planes? "

" B-25's are the only bombers with enough range. Will you take these fliers up to Hirohito's front yard and launch them to hit Tokyo? "

He gave that careful thought. " Thanks for the chance. Now

fill me in, please. Who will run the Air Force side of the show?"

On March 31 he was in San Francisco conferring with Lieutenant Colonel James Doolittle. "How are you going to lift loaded bombers off a tossing, bobbing flight deck?" Halsey wondered.

"For several months we've been practicing that. As you know, the proper ship speed can be a considerable help. My pilots can get airborne in a maximum of eight hundred feet — which," Doolittle added dryly, "we know is all you have.

"Our bombers are stripped of everything we can get along without," he went on. "That includes radio, because this won't be a talkfest anyway. We have five-man crews instead of eight. We won't carry the Norden bombsight, can't risk the Japs getting their hands on it. We'll use a new, cheap little gadget. And we'll fly in low. Admiral, how close to Japan can you take us?"

"Four hundred miles," Halsey said. "Of course, if the enemy spots us sooner, your crates will have to take off, wherever we may be." He added, "Without radio, your men stand little chance of getting back to the carrier. What happens after they drop their eggs?"

Doolittle avoided his look. "That part is a little ticklish. We won't come back to the carriers. We'll fly on over Japan, the Yellow Sea, and into China. Already our agents there have people scratching out airfields. The nearest will be at Yu-Shan."

"Yu-Shan? How far is that beyond Tokyo?"

"About fourteen hundred miles."

Halsey gave a low whistle. "Colonel Doolittle, I take off my hat to you and your men. What you're going to attempt takes an awful lot of guts."

Alameda Air Base, outside San Francisco, provided a shipping point for the sixteen B-25's in the project. Working fast, crews rolled the big bombers to the closely guarded Navy dock where they were derricked aboard the fleet's new carrier, the

*Hornet.* Her regular complement of aircraft were stored on the hangar deck, the bombers being lashed with wire ropes to her flight deck. Only Halsey and Doolittle knew their destination; even Captain Marc Mitscher, commander of the *Hornet,* would not know where he was taking these bombers until he opened sealed orders at sea.

As Task Force 18, the *Hornet,* two cruisers, and four destroyers were to steam a long north-circle course to rendezvous with Halsey's Task Force 16. Takeoff from the *Hornet* on April 12, it was calculated, should let the bombers reach Tokyo about dusk, and if all went well, reach China at dawn.

Several days of heavy weather off California prevented Halsey's flight back to Pearl Harbor and it became necessary to signal Mitscher for a one-day postponement of their April 12 rendezvous. Meanwhile, feverish and aching from influenza, Halsey refused to be hospitalized, and stuffing himself with cold pills, took the first plane flight available. He slept the entire way and stepped down at Pearl with his flu cured.

In addition to Task Force 16, Halsey now assumed responsibility as Commander Carriers Pacific Fleet, or COMCARDIV 2. This gave him direction of TF 18, the *Hornet* and her escorts, as well as his own TF 16. Once at sea his signal to the *Hornet* verified their meeting place off Kamchatka in the Bering Sea. Certain now that no leak was possible to the enemy, he announced to all ships' crews in 16:

"This force is bound for Tokyo."

The two task forces met and joined. Pausing in open ocean a thousand miles from Japan, the heavy ships refueled. Destroyers were left to guard the tanker, the safety of which was crucial to the big ships getting back to Pearl, and the two carriers and four cruisers began their run-in at twenty-three knots.

Radio silence was observed. Radar beams constantly swept the wintry ocean. The second night Halsey was roused from sleep at 0300, and hurrying to flag plot, was told,

"Radar blips show vessels, Admiral. Might be enemy pickets."

A change of course avoided these vessels, but four hours later another was recorded six miles away. Fearful that his force had been seen, Halsey ordered the light cruiser *Nashville* to sink her. A patrol boat, she proved elusive and with shells from eight-inch rifles digging water spouts around her, kept her radio crackling. At last three direct hits blew her to fragments.

Halsey groaned. "By now everybody in Japan must know about us. What is our position?"

Instead of the hoped-for four hundred miles from Tokyo, the squadron was still six hundred eighty-eight. Thought of the Doolittle planes risking that additional flight distance to safety in China made Halsey groan again. Because of that Japanese boat, in a few hours a considerable part of the Imperial Fleet would probably come steaming over the horizon.

He had no choice. At 0800 on April the eighteenth he radioed *Hornet:*

LAUNCH PLANES X TO COL DOOLITTLE AND HIS GALLANT COMMAND GOOD LUCK AND GOD BLESS YOU

The strong, cutting wind that drove green seas over the *Hornet's* ramp made takeoff of the heavily loaded bombers extremely hazardous. With hundreds of binoculars trained from other ships and the *Hornet's* entire crew assembled to watch, Doolittle's big plane was wheeled to the mark. His brakes gripping hard, he pulled his throttles to full power. With engines howling, the B-25 strained to go, vibrating as if she would shake apart. All of a sudden the brakes released. She lunged forward. In seconds she attained top speed and on the *Hornet's* lazy up-toss, hurtled out over the bow. When she fluttered down toward the reaching waves not an onlooker dared to breathe. Somehow the bomber recovered and began to climb.

The men of the whole task force cheered.

Plane after plane raced down the flight deck, faltered in stormy air currents over the water but clawed their way higher, higher. Just past the ramp, one paused on the brink of a stall. Several thousand men stood like statues, watching the pilot fight his controls. She steadied, began her painful climb.

Every bomber got safely airborne. Within an hour sixteen B-25's were diminishing dots in the slate sky.

On the *Big E*'s bridge the duty officer made a cryptic entry in her log: "Commencing retirement from area, course 090 at 25 knots."

Japanese-language interpreters monitored shipboard radios that were tuned to Tokyo stations. Later they heard a ball-bearing-voiced announcer boast that of all the nations at war, Japan was the only one whose homeland was safe from attack. Any foe daring to approach her shores, he assured, would be annihilated by the Emperor's invincible navy. The happy Japanese people could devote their attention to today's Festival of Cherry Blossoms. They could attend the championship baseball game, or they could –

He was cut off. Air-raid sirens were heard screaming in Tokyo streets. Lieutenant Colonel Doolittle's raiders had arrived.

It was sunny as the B-25's neared shore, flying at only thirty feet to elude detection and at slow speed to conserve gasoline. White sandy beaches passed below them, giving way to rolling green fields. Fruit trees were in bloom. Japanese farmers working neat gardenlike plots straightened to gaze upward. Sweeping nearer came Tokyo Bay with its edges a continuous tangle of docks and shipping. An aircraft carrier riding at anchor offered no objection to the visiting bombers. A flight of six Zero fighters roaming over the city altered their course for a closer look. One pilot waved as the B-25's sailed serenely on their way.

Beyond the bay stretched miles and miles of this city of paper-walled houses for eight million people. A school was letting out and hundreds of children paused in the street to wave handkerchiefs and caps at the aircraft. As yet there was no alarm.

The squadron divided. One flight group made for north Tokyo, one for its center, one for its southern part. Another headed for Yokohama and the Yokosuka Navy Yard. Still another flight turned south for the cities of Nagoya, Osaka, and Kobe.

Each plane carried four five-hundred-pound bombs. They were to be dropped on specified targets. Each pilot knew how many seconds of flight at a given speed would take him from the coastline to Target One, then to Target Two, and so on. He knew from photographs exactly what his targets looked like. Resembling a familiar motion picture, Tokyo unreeled below as each grim B-25 went about her errand.

As a target swam nearer, a plane climbed to fifteen hundred feet. This was to avoid being wrecked by the blast of her own high explosive. If enough distance remained before her next target, she dropped again to rooftop level. One by one, objectives were checked off. A tank factory received its bomb, a shipyard another, an aircraft plant a third. All bombs gone, the crews threw out packs of incendiary sticks. They fell apart in the air, and on striking any object, burst into three-hundred-degree flame, starting fires at steel plants, powder factories, arsenals, railroad yards, and oil refineries.

After the first wave the Tokyo raiders were brought under heavy AA attack, but not one received damage. The excited Japanese shot down one of their own barrage balloons. Of some thirty pursuit plane defenders, none were effective. B-25 gunners shot three out of the sky. The dense columns of smoke that rose in all parts of the city were American calling cards. An hour later the raid on Kobe proved a similar complete surprise.

It was after they left Tokyo that hazards piled up for Doolittle's men. One plane, dangerously low on fuel, headed northwest for Siberia. She managed to land near Vladivostok where the Russians interned her crew, but months later they escaped to China. Two other planes were forced to come down in China near Japanese positions. Their crews were taken prisoner.

For the others, after crossing the narrow waist of Japan they ran into violent electrical storms over the southern Sea of Japan. Ahead, there remained the tip of Korea and the Yellow Sea to traverse. To buck the strong winds cost extra gasoline from reserves already low. It was every bomber for herself, and the planes became scattered.

Night came on. Some of the B-25's found themselves still over the sea — but, their navigators questioned, what sea? Others were over land — but was it Japan, Korea, or China? There were no lights, no cities to be seen, no landing fields. Below, there was only stormy sea or desolate, craggy mountains. Some crews took a vote: Shall we bail out? Or stay with her till she goes down coughing on the last cupful of gas?

In pitch darkness at six thousand feet over an unknown land, the majority of crewmen bailed out. Most, landing in Free China, were received with kindness by poor farmers and fishermen. As best they could these folk attended the strangers' injuries and by signs and smiles showed their high opinion of China's ally, the United States. One flier was killed in landing. Eight others who found themselves in the Japanese-occupied part of China were captured. Six of these were beheaded with swords and the other two were never accounted for. Seventy of the seventy-nine crewmen of the B-25's eventually got back to America.

The Doolittle raid frightened Japanese military leaders. They decided to keep ready at home stronger land, sea, and air forces. How could they know when follow-up raids might come from the same source? And was that source China? Or an aircraft carrier? Or some Pacific island — say Midway? Damage to Tokyo and nearby cities, while considerable, was not enough to cripple Japan's war effort, but serious damage had been done to her morale.

In the United States the news that Emperor Hirohito's capital city had been attacked was electrifying. From where, people speculated, had Doolittle's fliers taken off on their mission? When reporters put the question to President Roosevelt he kept the secret of Task Force 16 by naming a fictional land supposed to be somewhere in Asia among the towering Himalayas.

"Our bombers," the President said with a wink, "took off from Shangri-La."

[Chapter 5]

# First Command

THE HALSEY NAME was known in America as early as 1637 in the Dutch colony of Nieuw Amsterdam. A Thomas Halsey lingered there awhile, but finding a town of six hundred people too crowded for his taste, left to carve a farm out of the wilderness of Long Island. Near Southampton a dozen years later, after his wife, Phoebe, was scalped by Indians, Thomas moved across the Sound to Connecticut. Evidently becoming some kind of official, he set people's taxes and did surveying to establish boundary lines.

Returning after a few years to his Long Island farm, Thomas Halsey was forever, his neighbors said, involved in disputes over land ownership, fences, and cattle. Often he conducted his " lawing " with fists and clubs. In his later years he battled for what he considered to be his rights less often with muscles and more often in court.

Down the march of generations other Halseys displayed similar combative spirit — big, vigorous men all, familiar with adventure. Many were seafarers and of these the most colorful was Captain John Halsey. Commissioned in 1704 by the Governor of Massachusetts to operate his ship as a privateer — that is, a licensed private warship — Captain John sailed about capturing not only enemy vessels but also any friendly ones that looked valuable.

This was piracy. Some of Captain John's adventures were

recorded in a long-forgotten book, *A History of the Robberies and Murders of the Most Notorious Pirates.* On one occasion, the book said, Captain John Halsey's brigantine engaged four ships at the same time and captured two of them. The booty, when sold, brought a quarter of a million dollars – in buying power about eight times that of today. In 1716 a fever claimed Captain John, who " died regretted by his own people " and was buried in a watermelon patch on the island of Madagascar.

Seafaring among the Halseys apparently ran aground for a hundred years until in 1815 Eliphalet Halsey commanded a Long Island whaler on a three-year voyage around Cape Horn. Over the next decades several others bearing the family name were whaling vessel masters.

The son of a New Jersey clergyman, William Frederick Halsey entered the United States Naval Academy in 1869. Just before the end of his four years of study he narrowly avoided dismissal for " Frenching out " – going to town without permission; but he was graduated, and over a thirty-five-year Navy career rose to the rank of captain.

His son, also William Frederick, was born in Elizabeth, New Jersey, on October 30, 1882.

When, from time to time, the Navy Department transferred young Halsey's father to a new tour of duty, occasionally across the nation, Mrs. Halsey, Bill, and his sister Deborah followed to be as near Dad as possible. As a result Bill attended schools in Coronado and Vallejo in California, Swarthmore in Pennsylvania, St. John's and Naval Academy Prep in Maryland, and the University of Virginia. Twice during those years, at the cost of black eyes and bruises, he persuaded schoolmates not to call him by the hated name " Willie."

Ambitious to become a Navy officer like his father, when Bill was nearing fifteen he felt ready for the Academy. A young man could be admitted only by obtaining one of the appointments allotted to each United States senator and congressman. The President also could make a few. The Halseys had lived many places, but in none long enough to become friendly with a senator or congressman or any helpful politician. Nobody would appoint young Bill.

He appealed by letter to President McKinley. His father, Bill wrote, was navigation officer of the U.S.S. *Montgomery*. " As you know, . . . Naval officers have not much influence." He was familiar, he said, with the Navy and ships, having lived three years at the Academy while his father was assigned there as a teacher; he knew and was known to " plenty of respectable people "; and his parents approved his choice of career if he could only obtain an appointment. Tactfully Bill ended his letter with congratulations on McKinley's recent election, " which every American sees is for the best."

He mailed this to the President and waited. There was no reply.

His father, optimistic that sooner or later an appointment could somehow be obtained, had Bill enter Naval Academy Preparatory School in Annapolis. A year passed; still no appointment. A second year. Bill was now nearing seventeen. At last he decided that next best to being a Navy officer would be to become a doctor, so he enrolled in the University of Virginia medical school at Charlottesville. There was faint hope that, like Leonard Wood, who had entered the Army as a physician and risen to be a general, Bill would be accepted by the Navy as a doctor and after that somehow earn a command.

At Charlottesville he joined a fraternity and proceeded to devote more energy to football than to studies. Too light and not good enough to make the varsity, he played left end on the scrubs. In the last practice before the important game with Georgetown University he tackled the star quarterback too hard and the gentleman suffered a broken leg.

Suddenly Bill Halsey was the most unpopular man at the University of Virginia. There were even dark hints about a lynching. Gloomily he was debating whether to quit school when, to his surprise, the coach included him in the squad traveling to Washington. Huddled on the bench there, Bill daydreamed of going in and scoring the winning touchdown against Georgetown. That would have been the way of things in a story, but he did not get into the game.

After a pleasant year at Virginia he still yearned to win an appointment to the Naval Academy. "You are sure?" his mother asked. Yes, he was positive.

A quiet-mannered lady, when justice seemed to go off the track Mrs. Halsey could be very tenacious about putting it back on the rails. She took a train to Washington. Chin high, she marched straight to the White House. Coolly she sailed past a cordon of startled secretaries and presently found herself seated across a desk from President William McKinley.

She explained her need, pointing out that soon young Bill Halsey would be too old to enter the Naval Academy. It was unfair, she declared, that a distinguished officer like her husband, now in his second tour of duty on the Academy faculty, had no means of helping his son to follow the same patriotic career.

Mrs. Halsey left the White House with an appointment for Bill written in the President's hand.

Several times as a fourth-year, third-year, then second-year cadet Bill came near "bilging out" of the Academy. His studies record was poor. Just before one examination in theoretical mechanics his grade was 2.28 of a possible 4.00. This was on the brink of flunking and his father sternly advised that Bill give up football.

"Sir," Bill replied, "I'd rather bilge out."

Top scholars in his class tutored him and several others weak in the subject far into the night. Next day after the examination Bill walked over to his father's quarters for lunch.

Lieutenant Halsey was waiting anxiously in the doorway. "Have the marks been posted?"

"Yes, sir."

"Well, what did you get?"

"I got 3.98, sir."

His father shook his head and turned away. "Apparently," he mourned, "you have been drinking."

In football Bill did not advance beyond the scrubs for two years, but just before the 1902 season the Naval Academy's regular fullback was injured. Halsey was sent in as a substitute and managed to hold the position until he was graduated. It was, however, one of the Navy's weakest teams, losing both seasons by one-sided scores to their bitter rival, Army. Years later in Washington, General Eisenhower, introducing himself as "Army's worst halfback," asked to shake hands with "the man who claims to be Navy's worst fullback."

Summer cruises helped to develop cadets into real sailormen. As each one began, some queasy unfortunates "went by rail," but in all his career Bill Halsey was not once seasick. It was an age when sailing vessels were becoming fewer and steamships more numerous and the beginners were required to be thoroughly familiar with both. As a third classman Bill was proud to be made royal yardman on the steamer-schooner *Chesapeake*. Two years later he held the second most responsible cadet post, port captain of the maintop on the same ship, now commanded by his father.

During one cruise Bill and several shipmates, to prove their sea-dogginess, endured tattooing crudely done by a coal passer. The design, drawn by one of their number, was a fouled anchor with "USNA" across its crown and its chain forming "04." Very soon Bill realized that it had been foolish to become thus gaudily branded for life.

Under President Theodore Roosevelt our Navy was expanding so rapidly that Halsey's class was graduated in February instead of June to help man the new ships. One third of the original ninety-three cadets had been dropped along the way, and of those who survived, scholastically Bill Halsey stood forty-third. At any rate he was at last a Passed Midshipman.

His career began on one battleship *Missouri* and forty years later ended on another. Indicating the vast changes in fighting ships over that period, the early *Missouri's* crew was six hundred fifty-two men, the later one's over twenty-six hundred; the first displaced twelve thousand five hundred tons and the later one forty-five thousand. The first was nicknamed "Mizzy," but the awesome might of the second caused her to be dubbed "Mighty Mo."

After two years of apprenticeship a midshipman was commissioned an ensign. Ensign Halsey served aboard the *Don Juan de Austria,* onetime yacht of the queen of Spain, raised after the Spanish-American War from the bottom of Manila Bay. Now a gunboat, the *Don Juan* was assigned to Caribbean waters. She made various cruises, her guns once providing authority for American customs collectors to function in Santo Domingo to get a loan repaid. Later for six dull months she sat at anchor in baking-hot Samana Bay.

To demonstrate to the world that America now was a first-class naval power, President Theodore Roosevelt assembled our Atlantic Fleet under Admiral Robley Evans for a tour of the globe. The sixteen battleships and five destroyers were painted white to indicate our peaceful intentions and the Fleet, with Ensign Halsey aboard the *Kansas*, was off for a nearly two-year cruise. It steamed down the east coast of South America, through the Straits of Magellan and up the West Coast to San Diego. There, Halsey was leading his company in a street parade when a small boy pointed at him, exclaiming, "Look, Ma, he has a face like a bulldog."

The cruise continued to Hawaii, Australia, the Philippines, and Japan. Each hospitable port vied with the others in offering bigger parties and celebrations, and sometimes officers and crew were glad to put to sea to recuperate.

In Japan, Halsey was among a score of officers attending a party aboard Admiral Count Heihachiro Togo's flagship, the *Mikasa.* Desiring to pay the most distinguished of the guests their highest compliment, six young Japanese officers seized

Ambassador O'Brien and Admiral Sperry and tossed them in the air amid shouts of "*Banzai!*" Promptly this friendly gesture was imitated by the Americans, who tossed up Admiral Togo. Thirty-three years later Halsey regretted that the admiral had not accidentally been thrown overboard.

In peacetime, Navy life largely consisted of cruises, training exercises, waiting, more exercises, waiting, being transferred, more cruises, and several years apart, promotions.

An ambitious officer tried to prepare himself, particularly during off-duty hours at sea, for the rigorous examinations that preceded each promotion. After two years as ensign Halsey was ordered to Washington, where he took oral and written examinations for six days of eight hours each. They were in such subjects as ordnance and gunnery, marine and electrical engineering, international law, navigation and seamanship. He passed and was made a lieutenant junior grade. Normally he would have held this rank at least two years, but because of the need at that time for officers, he held it only a few minutes, then was promoted to full lieutenant.

In 1909 occurred two of the most important events in Bill Halsey's life. One was assuming his first command, the second, assuming the role of husband.

At the Charleston Navy Yard, half a dozen rusty and dejected-looking hulks included the ancient torpedo boat *Dupont.* In the eyes of every young officer the vessel that is his first command looms impressive, however crippled and drab she may actually be. When the national colors and the commissioning pennant rippled over the *Dupont,* Halsey drew a long breath. She was beautiful! Time and her frequent breakdowns gradually weakened this conviction.

Three years earlier aboard the *Don Juan de Austria,* while drilling a squad on deck he had showed off a little to impress an attractive young lady who stood watching with the executive officer and his wife. She found Halsey's manner so irritating that on impulse she cocked back her arm and hurled her fur muff at him. It knocked his cap over the ship's side. His men burst out laughing. Halsey, red-faced, barked, "Dismissed!" He refused to give back the girl's muff until she told him her name, Frances Cooke Grandy of Norfolk.

As their acquaintance ripened, Halsey learned that an uncle of hers had been engineer on the Confederate *Merrimac* during the historic Civil War battle in Hampton Roads with the United States ironclad *Monitor*. Further, some of her southern relatives seemed to hold Halsey personally responsible for the entire war. But he was not courting her relatives and in December of 1909 he married Frances Grandy.

From the *Dupont* he was transferred to the destroyer *Lamson*, to the training ship *Franklin*, to the destroyer *Flusser*. Gradually rising in rank, except for a twelve months' tour as executive officer of the battleship *Wyoming*, all Bill Halsey's sea duty over the next twenty-three years was spent aboard destroyers.

[Chapter 6]

# World War I

THE OUTBREAK of war in Europe in 1914 brought increased activity for our Navy, even though the United States was not involved. To make sure our neutrality was respected, patrols kept constant watch along the Atlantic seaboard.

Destroyers were used freely in such patrolling, and in bad weather their continual crisscross of main-traveled sea-lanes to our ports could be hazardous. During one six-hundred-mile cruise off busy New York harbor Halsey's orders called for his current command, the *Jarvis,* to follow a succession of zigzagging courses at stated speeds. Heavy cloud cover lasting several days prevented his taking a celestial fix to determine his exact whereabouts. He could only proceed depending on log and compass, a method sailors call dead reckoning.

With lookouts doubled, the *Jarvis* knifed through the water at twelve knots. Unable to penetrate the murk, Halsey on the bridge suddenly felt urgent warning of danger. At his order, "Full speed astern!" her racing engines pulled the *Jarvis* to a stop. She lay rolling in the semidarkness. There was no sound above the lap of waves along her side.

Off her port rail a low blur proved to be a man in a fishing dory. Halsey called, "Can you tell me my position?"

"This is shoal water," came the reply. "Keep straight ahead another half mile and you'll knock over the Fire Island Lifesaving Station."

Instinct or some vague feeling of change in his ship's condition had saved the *Jarvis* and perhaps many lives. Only years of experience at sea could develop that sensitivity in a commander.

Transferred the next year to the Naval Academy, Halsey found himself heading its discipline department. The cadets were much the same barrel of monkeys his own class had been, constantly testing the regulations and feeling great pride when they could evade them without detection. Smoking was the commonest infraction, and one student genius rigged some kind of smoke-consuming device in his shower that Halsey knew was there but never could lay hands on. Another, an electrical wizard, contrived a hidden central control of all the bells, lights, and elevators in Bancroft Hall. He amused himself by switching them on and off to create confusion until, probably feeling the search for him beginning to close in, he desisted.

A combination detective and judge, Bill Halsey tried to be understanding, but imposed severe punishment on miscreants. As to smoking, he believed the rule needlessly harsh and advised that it be relaxed.

Although he found this work interesting, when the United States entered the war in 1917 Halsey, now a lieutenant commander, hoped every telephone call would mean the Navy Department was ordering him to duty with the Fleet. Through a friend in Washington he learned his name was on a list of officers requested to serve under Admiral William Sims, commander of our naval forces in Europe, and at once Halsey applied to the Commandant of Midshipmen to be detached.

In Queenstown, Ireland, in January, 1918, he reported for duty aboard the destroyer *Duncan.* A month later, promoted to temporary commander, he became skipper of the *Benham.*

Queenstown was the base for English and American warships charged with safeguarding convoys of merchant vessels and tankers. Off some Irish, English, or French port, the *Ben-*

*ham,* with half a dozen other destroyers and a cruiser or two, would meet a dozen or fifteen merchantmen and shepherd them westward five hundred miles. Once past the operating limit of most German submarines, the warships turned away to pick up another convoy eastbound for Europe, loaded with munitions and supplies.

The work had a certain tense monotony in summer and grueling discomfort in stinging North Atlantic gales all winter. The four-stack, thin-skinned destroyers of the day were too long and too narrow of beam to be comfortable ships, always tossing and pitching and with so little freeboard that in a storm, icy green seas swept their decks. Often for two or three days at a time the *Benham,* and later the *Shaw,* bucked so that hot food could not be prepared. Often the weather or repeated submarine alerts kept Bill Halsey on his bridge twenty-four hours at a stretch.

The days and weeks ground past. Periscopes low in the water were difficult to see, and now and then in spite of the guard ships' vigilance, U-boats crept into the midst of a convoy. A speeding streak of foam could be the only warning before a torpedo bored into a hull with a tremendous explosion. A ten-thousand-ton merchantman mortally hurt could slide stern-first below the waves in minutes, leaving her crew to struggle in near-freezing water.

When a ship was torpedoed, others in the convoy dared not pause for rescue lest they too be hit. It was Navy's task to pick up survivors and to hunt down the enemy. Destroyers raced about the ocean like terriers, dropping depth charges where the U-boat was thought to be. Some torpedo wakes turned out to be only wave crests and some periscopes only floating spars, but in moments of danger there was no time for close inspection. Once the *Shaw*'s exploding "ash cans" brought up an oil slick and she received credit for a "probable" U-boat victim.

One day the *Shaw* suddenly came upon a submarine just

surfacing four hundred yards off her bow, a plain target. At the lookout's cry, "Sub dead ahead!" Halsey rushed to the bridge. The crew of his forward deck gun were already at stations, the pointer's finger poised above his trigger. This submarine, Halsey vowed, he would certainly sink. But the quartermaster beside him, telescope at his eye, called out, "Hold it, sir! This one's American."

Certain other moments of excitement held more humor and made good telling later in cozy wardrooms. At Queenstown when the *Benham* was casting off, the deck officer reported, "All lines clear." But a hawser strung by a repair crew still ran from a stern cleat under projecting depth charge guns to a bollard on the dock. At "Slow speed ahead" the *Shaw* advanced and lunged obliquely at the vessel moored next to her. Somehow Halsey avoided a crash; then his ship, like a bulldog straining at its leash, lunged the other way at a sister destroyer. Attempting to put to sea while your command is still tied to the dock can give any skipper his career's most embarrassing moment.

Off Ireland another day, lookouts reported phosphorescence in the water: air bubbles from a surfacing sub? The General Alarm clattered. Grimly Halsey believed this time he had trapped a U-boat, and when the phosphorescent area widened he judged the enemy to be crash-diving. With his hand raised to signal to let go depth charges off the stern, he took another glance over the port rail. The water was alive with a school of fish.

In August, 1918, Halsey was sent to Philadelphia to command the new twelve-hundred-ton *Yarnall.*

Two weeks before the *Yarnall* was commissioned, World War I came to an end in the signing of the Armistice between Germany and the Allies. This caused Halsey to be held in the States. Soon the *Yarnall* got her shakedown cruise as an escort to the liner *George Washington* on which President Wilson went to Europe to attend the Peace Conference.

Over the following six months Halsey was kept busy ferrying important persons across the Channel, called "the seasick circuit," between England and France. He also led an Allied board to inspect German submarine bases and took part in receiving the surrender of German Navy and merchant ships. This accomplished, he was sent on a cruise to Lisbon.

In the spring of 1919 three Navy seaplanes took off from Newfoundland in a pioneering attempt to fly to England by way of the Azores and Portugal. With the *Yarnall* acting as one of several picket ships along their route, Halsey saw the NC-4, the only plane to complete the trip, pass overhead. This historic flight eight years before Lindbergh's nonstop solo trip to Europe was a trailblazer for today's hundreds of daily Atlantic crossings by air.

After the *Yarnall* escorted President Wilson, again aboard the *George Washington*, back to the United States, she was posted to the newly formed Pacific Fleet. When the Fleet sailed for the Panama Canal, Halsey had his first command of a division of six destroyers. At San Diego his ship, with a number of others, was ordered to the China Station, but he remained behind as skipper of the *Chauncey*.

Before he took command of the *Benham* at Queenstown she had been in a collision. After he left the *Shaw* the liner *Aquitania* surged out of fog to chop ninety feet off her bow. But in eleven years spent at sea no vessel he commanded had been involved in more than a paint-scraping rub against a dock. Apprehension kept mounting in Halsey that such an extraordinary run of luck must end, and on a cruise to Pearl Harbor the next spring it did.

In mid-Pacific, without warning, the *Chauncey*'s engine-room telegraph rang "Stop." Water in her boilers had abruptly fallen so low that to avoid an explosion her tubes had to be blown. Other destroyers were fanned out in her wake, the nearest the *Aaron Ward*. Halsey had no steam for warning blasts of his whistle. He ordered the breakdown flag run up, a signal that a ship is out of control, but a strong wind from astern fouled it in the foremast rigging.

An ensign who had the conn on the *Aaron Ward* saw the *Chauncey* lose way. Not fully appreciating the danger, he reduced speed by one third and kept coming. The *Chauncey*, without power, without even steering control, lay dead in the water.

At about five knots the *Aaron Ward* smashed through the *Chauncey*'s propeller guard and continued into her steering engine room. It flooded. The *Ward*'s bow cut the starboard wire to the tiller and disabled the starboard engine. No one was injured. Still afloat and able to limp along, the *Chauncey* eventually reached Pearl Harbor.

For a Fleet exercise off California months later, Halsey was given command of three destroyer divisions of six vessels each, with a nineteenth for his flagship. His squadron was to start the exercise thirty thousand yards away and simulate a torpedo attack on four battleships.

Working out his strategy, Halsey formed two of his destroyer divisions into single files a thousand yards apart. In case the battleships' course proved out of their reach he kept his third division at ready.

On the day of the exercise, leading his two divisions in lines, he verified that he would soon intercept the battleships and ordered his dozen destroyers to make heavy smoke. With this concealment of their movements, he succeeded in luring the battlewagons between his two lines, which then "attacked" them from both sides.

As the leading destroyers closed to three thousand yards, each fired two torpedoes. Their nonexplosive practice heads were made of soft metal calculated to do no damage. But Halsey's tactic kept his destroyers rapidly closing the range until his ships at the ends of his lines were firing from only seven hundred yards. This consumed little of the torpedoes' compressed-air propulsion, and they made smashing impact.

One torpedo penetrated the hull of the *New Mexico,* flagship of the admiral commanding the exercise. Immediately she began to take water. Two torpedoes striking the *Mississippi's* propellers bent them into steel pretzels. She was forced to call for a tow to the nearest drydock. A direct hit under the engine room of the *Texas* knocked out most electrical controls and left her all but helpless.

Next morning a summons brought Halsey aboard the *New Mexico.* He climbed her boarding stairs chesty and smiling, expecting praise for yesterday's success. Instead, he found himself facing a red-faced, snarling vice admiral.

"Commander, do you realize what your confounded antics are going to cost the United States Navy?"

Shaken, Halsey managed, "No, sir."

The admiral took up a paper and waved it. "By this estimate, the damage you did to our battleships yesterday will amount to a million and a half dollars!"

Bill Halsey's knees felt watery. Was he going to be court-martialed?

The admiral took to pacing his cabin. "Of course, I admit your strategy was brilliant. You did the unexpected. You did it well, then got away from there fast." Still scowling, he offered his hand. "In tomorrow's exercise you will fire from no nearer than five thousand yards. Is that understood? It will be a lot cheaper."

A Navy officer's career consists of successive tours of duty, now at sea, now on land. Each tour is calculated to broaden his experience and value to the service. If in time he rises to captain or higher, he has proved himself capable of assuming almost any responsibility of his profession. In sea duty most officers are rotated among destroyers, cruisers, and battleships and sometimes submarines. It was unusual that Halsey's experience so far had been limited to destroyers.

However, a variety of other assignments remained. He made his permanent rank as commander in June, 1921. Posted to

Intelligence in the Navy Department in Washington, he became skipper of an LSD – a large steel desk. After a year of the paper work that Halsey disliked, he then went to Germany as naval attaché to Ambassador Houghton. After two years he returned to sea on the bridge of the destroyer *Dale,* then the *Osborne,* both kept in European waters to show the flag. Back in the United States, he got his first battlewagon experience as executive officer of the *Wyoming.*

With his promotion to captain, Halsey was ordered back to the Naval Academy. There he commanded the onetime cruiser *Reina Mercedes* which, like the old *Don Juan de Austria,* had been salvaged from the bottom of Manila Bay after the Spanish-American War. Now a receiving ship, the *Mercedes* provided comfortable quarters for Halsey and his family. She was also a dormitory for instructors and a prison ship for errant midshipmen. All Academy floating equipment was in Halsey's charge – sailboats, cutters, rowboats, powerboats, even buoys. For three and a half years this pleasant responsibility permitted him ample time for sociability in Annapolis and nearby Baltimore and Washington.

In 1927 the *Mercedes* also became the base for the first aviation detail assigned to the Academy. As this too was under Halsey's command he thought he ought to learn about it. He asked Lieutenant DeWitt Ramsey, "Why not educate me?" Ramsey took him on several flights, and when he permitted his passenger to handle the controls, Bill Halsey became fascinated.

"Aviation represents our next big change in warfare," he told his wife. "Somehow I've got to get into this!"

Many of his officer friends derided the idea that aviation would ever become important to the Navy. At the luncheon table and in wardrooms the discussions went on for hours. At Malta, Halsey had seen England's first aircraft carrier and although it looked ungainly, he believed carrier design would be perfected to offer a powerful new arm of the Fleet.

"No, no, Bill. Carriers are a waste of taxpayers' money," one officer scoffed. "Nothing can slug it out like a battleship. As for planes, can you imagine depending on flying coffins for your protection?"

Ever since the war, controversy had raged between the Navy and the Army Air Service as to the airplane's military value. Air Service men led by General William Mitchell called the airplane the ultimate weapon. But battleship commanders and even Secretary of the Navy Daniels insisted that planes could be useful only for reconnaissance.

The fiery Billy Mitchell managed to awaken the American public to the argument, and when he openly challenged the Navy to a test, there could be no refusal. Two captured German vessels, a battleship and a cruiser, were anchored in the Atlantic a hundred miles off the Virginia capes. The *Ostfriesland*, the Navy vowed, was unsinkable by aerial bombs. Secretary Daniels even offered to stand on her bridge while Mitchell's Martin bombers rained down their six-hundred-pounders.

It was fortunate the Secretary remained only a spectator because on their first run the bombers sank the cruiser *Ostfriesland*.

"That was a setup," explained red-faced Navy men. "If those ships could have fired back, Mitchell's birds would never have got close enough to drop bombs. They'd have been shot down like clay pigeons."

Clay pigeons, Halsey countered, could not shoot back. But aircraft could.

His belief in Naval aviation steadily increasing, he applied in 1930 for pilot training. When he failed the physical examination because of weakness of one eye he was disconsolate. "With this in my record," he told his wife gloomily, "I'll never get out of destroyers. In fact I'll be lucky if they keep me. I'm practically walking the plank right now."

He was assigned to command a squadron of nineteen destroyers with the Atlantic Fleet. There his belief in the possibilities of military flying gained new strength as he noted the wasted uses of the one or two planes some battleships carried. Never welcomed, only tolerated, they were permitted to observe from aloft gunnery practice results and torpedo runs. One battleship sent her plane off to scout, then her executive officer forgot to meet it at the agreed rendezvous. The pilot was down to his last gallon of fuel when he managed a safe landing in Haiti.

Halsey's next transfer was ashore, to the Naval War College at Newport, Rhode Island. For a year he studied tactics and naval logistics, then moved on to be an exchange student at the Army War College in Washington. Not only battles were the concern here but entire wars from the viewpoint of the General Staff.

Bill Halsey had all but accepted the fact that for him the door to aviation was forever closed when a letter came from the Navy Bureau of Aeronautics. " I can offer you command of our new aircraft carrier *Saratoga*," Admiral Ernest King wrote in effect, " if you will first go through flight training as an observer."

Would he! That day he quit smoking. He began a strict diet to reduce his overweight. At fifty-one years of age Bill Halsey was at last in Naval Aviation.

[Chapter 7]

# Captain Cadet

THE OBSERVER and pilot trainees at Pensacola, Florida, Naval Air Station were mostly young ensigns. The officer in charge was a lieutenant commander. One day in walked a thirty-year Navy veteran who wore the four half-inch gold stripes of a captain of the line on his blue uniform sleeves and who was old enough to have been the father of anyone on the station.

Bill Halsey found that his first problem was to persuade his new associates, most of them five ranks below him, to accept him as an equal. He wanted no salutes, no coming to attention when he appeared, no " sirring," and no " Yes, Captain." When an instructor offered, " I'll have someone carry your parachute out to your plane, sir," Halsey exploded. " I'll carry my own confounded parachute! I'm only a cadet here like everyone else. Kindly treat me exactly the same, no better, no worse."

His insistence gradually won common consent to ignore his superior rank. Once this was accomplished, he found his age no bar to free companionship with younger men. A nationally syndicated newspaper columnist, however, learning of Halsey's assignment, wrote that because of his rank, he was being accorded " country club " treatment. He was exempt from all work hard enough to cause perspiration, this critic said, was flown here and there as he chose and in all ways received plush treatment. When Halsey tired of this " training," the skeptical columnist forecast, he would let the base commander know and forthwith would be awarded a shiny pair of wings.

Such distortion of facts enraged Bill Halsey. He wrote a scathing letter to be relayed to the columnist by the Navy Department, inviting the gentleman to come and sample the " country club " living. If he dared to, Halsey thought grimly, he would have the fellow taken through such aerial acrobatics that his stomach would never return to normal position. He heard no more about the matter.

The training was grueling, but to Halsey it held fascination. The beginners' squadron of observers spent every morning on the study of engines, radio, gunnery, bombing, and torpedoes. No one got dirtier or sweatier dismantling motors and putting them back together than Cadet Halsey. Afternoons, each trainee flew with an instructor to learn simple tactics and dead-stick (emergency) landings, and soon Halsey could tell by occasional scoldings for his clumsiness that he was completely accepted.

Much as he valued observer training, he still yearned to become a pilot. Not that he expected, at his age, to do much flying, but firsthand knowledge should make him a better commander of the *Saratoga*. He decided to keep this reasoning to himself and to omit mention that eye trouble had made him fail a physical examination for pilot training. He asked to be transferred, and was.

Pilot now of a land trainer, he learned about landings and takeoffs and keeping formation with other planes. On a cross-country flight his instructor passed a scribbled note: " Control is yours. Find our way home." Occupying the rear seat, Halsey discovered he could not read the compass mounted five feet ahead beyond the instructor's shoulder on the instrument panel.

For a moment he felt panic. He dared not confess to weak sight, which would immediately lead to his being washed out of training. Staring overside, he noticed railroad tracks below, which he reasoned must lead back to Pensacola. Halsey began to " fly by the iron compass." After a few miles the railroad forked. He chose the wrong branch.

While he flew this way and that, trying to get his bearings, the instructor sat grimly watchful, offering no comment. At sundown sheer luck brought Halsey to the airfield, and when the plane rolled to a stop, his instructor's saved-up remarks made his ears tingle.

Two ground crewmen trotted up. " Say, skipper, we were gettin' worried about you."

" We always worry about you," his buddy added.

He had as many mishaps as any other rookie flier. Coming in one day to land, he overshot his circle and found himself racing at eighty knots toward a fence. He faced the swift choice of smashing into it or ground-looping. He chose to ground-loop. The plane was not seriously damaged nor was Halsey. Crawling out from under, he counted his bruises and scratches and told himself, " Let this teach you not to be so cocky."

In the third stage of training he flew service planes, OU's such as were in use in carrier scouting squadrons. Again in a landing, a soft spot in the ground made his plane somersault with a tremendous crash. The control towerman sent a fire truck and an ambulance screaming to his aid. Inching free of the wreck, Halsey stood up, his legs rubbery, dazed, and with a two-inch cut in his forehead bleeding profusely. But when the ambulance men seized him to lay him on their stretcher, he wrenched out of their grasp.

" Where," he demanded, " is the operations officer? "

" Here." The man came running up. " Get on that stretcher. You're going to the hospital for a checkup."

" I'm all right. Look," Halsey appealed, " will you give me another plane? I've got to go back up there right now. Fly. So I won't lose my nerve."

The officer, ambulance men, and fire fighters exchanged glances. " All right," the officer yielded. " But, Halsey, I don't think there's much chance that you'll ever lose your nerve."

Soon he was handling fighter planes and learning the aerobatics that can mean the difference between life and death in high combat. He never became really skillful, he admitted, at tricks requiring a light touch on the stick, but in stunts " where you just kick the plane around " he managed to qualify.

A third bad landing when he failed to see a rope stretched between two poles convinced Bill Halsey that it would be sensible to wear glasses. Secretly he visited a Pensacola civilian doctor and had corrective lenses fitted into his goggles. No one on the base ever learned about his weak eye.

Squadron Five, the last stage of instruction, had a penalty for any flier who ran over and smashed one of the airfield boundary lights. Called the Flying Jackass, this award was an aluminum plate to strap on the flier's chest. It was a cutout of a donkey's head, and the erring pilot had to wear it on base at all times except when flying.

Halsey ingloriously earned the Flying Jackass by smashing a light, but over several days heard nothing about having to wear the emblem. The squadron commander felt that it might weaken discipline to have a Navy captain likened to a dunce before dozens of ensigns thirty years his junior. Halsey sought him out to protest.

" I'm no different," he insisted, " than anyone else."

With the squadron drawn up on parade, the mock formal ceremony was held to " decorate " Bill Halsey with the Flying Jackass. His classmates' boos were the loudest ever heard on the base. As he wore the long-eared breastplate for the next two weeks they made the most of this chance to hurl gibes at a superior officer. When another pilot ran over a boundary light, requiring transfer of the Jackass to him, Halsey asked to keep it.

" Make him another, will you? " he requested. " I want to hang this in my cabin on the *Saratoga*. Every time somebody does something stupid it will remind me, before I chew him out, that I'm none too bright myself."

For eleven months he continued to demand and receive " the

full treatment." Chancing to be the last man of the trainees to fly solo, he was seized and tossed into the ocean and came up sputtering to find forty ensigns laughing at him. Proudly he stood in line with them on graduation day to receive a certificate that rated him Naval Aviator and the wings insignia to prove it.

Mrs. Halsey joined him, startled to find her husband forty-five pounds thinner and seeming to believe he was back at age twenty-one. They devoted his short leave to motoring across the nation to Long Beach, where Bill Halsey got his heart's desire, command of an aircraft carrier, in the summer of 1935.

The *Lexington* and *Saratoga*, sister ships, were converted battle cruisers and the largest war vessels in the world. Although navigators called them "heavy" to maneuver, their 185,000 horsepower engines were ample for their tonnage. This power was great enough that when the lighting system failed in Tacoma, Washington, the *Lex* hooked up her dynamos with city cables and for a month delivered all the electricity Tacoma required.

Only once, aboard the battleship *Wyoming*, had Halsey had the experience of bringing a ship larger than a destroyer to harbor anchorage. Especially when wind and tides made a ship hard to control and other vessels were nearby, this could be a feat of seamanship. As a destroyer commander, Halsey had invented the startling technique of dropping anchor and rapidly paying out chain while he still steamed at cruise speed. Suddenly reversing engines full power, he could bring his craft to a shuddering halt precisely where he wanted her to be. Not a stunt, this was an effective maneuver to counteract unfavorable weather conditions.

Wondering if the mighty *Sara* could be handled similarly, he decided to find out. Carefully he instructed his executive officer in the necessary steps. The officer was aghast. "But, Captain, that's dangerous. The *Sara* is no tin can! You can't whip her around the way you do a destroyer."

"I think the difference is only a matter of size. We'll try a flying anchorage."

Word of the test spread among the crew. With every man tense and while watchers on other ships exclaimed, "Is the *Sara* out of control?" she entered busy Coronado Roads at a brisk nine knots. Her anchor splashed down but she kept coming.

"She's headed for the beach!" men cried.

Seventy-five fathoms of chain clattered out of her hawse hole, then suddenly it ceased running. The water at the *Sara*'s stern boiled with propellers reversing at full speed. Her anchor bit deep, and with a jerk like that of a bronco at the end of a lariat, she dipped her bow, rolled gently and stopped.

An admiral watching from his flagship mopped his perspiring brow. "It's that Halsey again! Everybody else in this Navy knows there are certain things you can't do. He goes out and does 'em."

Aboard the *Sara,* her skipper stood grinning at his white-faced executive officer. "The old girl seems to think she *is* a destroyer. What do you say we never tell her?"

For two years Bill Halsey commanded the *Saratoga* and later for two years while he was a rear admiral she was his flagship. He lived aboard her, he said, longer than he ever lived anywhere else.

There were cruises and Fleet exercises over the next several years — though not as many as Navy men desired because of meager appropriations by Congress. Transferred to Pensacola to command the Air Station where he had earned his wings, Halsey learned more about the use and mobility of aircraft in wartime. Made a rear admiral, lower half, he commanded Carrier Division 2, which consisted of the *Yorktown* and *Enterprise* in Caribbean maneuvers.

On leave in Norfolk, Virginia, Halsey saw a Navy yeoman run into the street and wave his car to a stop. The man handed him emergency orders to sail immediately for the West Coast. The suddenness of the move later appeared to have been based on an intelligence report that on July 1, 1939, Japan intended to blow up the Panama Canal.

Japan did not do so. Tension between the nations relaxed. In California the Admiral transferred his two-star blue flag from the *Yorktown* to the *Saratoga.*

During war games held jointly with the Army that fall, the Fleet played the role of an enemy protecting its invasion landing of an infantry division. The *Sara* operated independently and used her planes to harass defending airfields along the coast. The farthest distant of these was a bomber base two hundred miles inland at Reno, Nevada. Its commander considered it safely beyond attack range and did not bother to throw up planes on patrol.

Although the United States now had five aircraft carriers, this newest Fleet arm was still tolerated more than it was welcomed. Flag-rank officers almost to a man saw carrier planes as useful for scouting and, to a minor extent, for Fleet defense. But to win a battle or a war, they pointed out, you had to hunt down the enemy and smash him by sheer weight of striking power. No weapon had the might of a modern battleship, they insisted, and probably none ever would have. Yes, it was pleasant to have carrier planes to run little errands, but of course they lacked the power to destroy.

Bill Halsey could get red-faced and pound the table at this dim evaluation. To him a carrier was a floating bomber and fighter-plane airfield, with great striking power potential. Outargued in many a wardroom, he constantly sought opportunities to prove what a carrier would do. That Reno airfield was just such a challenge, and he immediately accepted it.

He sent the *Sara*'s fighters winging over the sea, shore, and mountains. Surprise at the Reno base was so complete and the mock strafing so heavy that not one plane could take the air in defense. Adding insult to injury, several of Halsey's pilots dropped parachutes with alarm clocks suspended, bearing notes that said, "Hey, Army! Time to wake up!"

Soon the *Sara* was in a group of ships under Admiral Pye and bound for Hawaii. The cruise provided no time for rest, only drill and again drill as Halsey constantly sought more efficient cooperation between his ship and her planes.

Familiar now with the handling of the ungainly-appearing carrier, he also knew firsthand the perils her pilots faced in takeoffs and landings. A combat pilot based ashore had to know how to fly, navigate, shoot, bomb, and how to operate a radio; the carrier-based flier had to know all this and more. He had to be alert lest his engine fail just as he shot over the ship's bow. If his wheels touched water, they would somersault his plane. He might be knocked unconscious. His safety belt might snag or his canopy might jam. Any of these could cost his life by drowning. Or, struggling in the water, he might be run over by his own ship.

To deal with these hazards called for thorough knowledge of a plane's capabilities and limitations. It required an understanding of air currents over water. It meant that maintenance of planes in prime operating condition was even more important here than it was on land. The safety and efficiency of aircraft carrier flying in all its aspects became an obsession with Halsey.

Two of his familiar problems had to do with communications. Each carrier had her own separate radio wavelength to her planes. Thus a scouting plane that sighted the enemy would radio word back to its mother ship. In turn the mother ship would radio the news to the task force flagship. The flagship would relay it to other vessels, whereupon each would notify her own planes aloft. The delay in all this, Halsey pointed out, might sometime prove disastrous. Why not have a common wavelength for a whole task force and all its planes?

The Navy, proud of its long and valiant history of service, was in some ways tradition-clogged. Any proposal for change brought quick, stubborn objection. "But we've always done it this way. It's always worked, hasn't it?" Many, many times

Halsey had proposed this change and as many times he had been squelched. Now he won the interest of Admiral Pye, who ordered the one-wavelength system carefully tested. It proved much faster in spreading crucial information and it reduced the number of errors inevitable in multiple relay transmission.

The second communications problem was related to the first. In each dive bomber and observation scout plane an observer rode behind the pilot to man a machine gun and to operate the radio. But there was a shortage of observers. Their training, which included study of the Morse code, extended over several months. Why not shorten this training by a matter of weeks, Halsey asked, by eliminating the study of Morse code? Why not, instead, use open-voice radio?

Trials at sea showed that voice transmission could not be jammed by an enemy any more easily than Morse. It was equally effective, according to weather, up to a hundred fifty miles.

TBS, talk between ships, became everyday Fleet usage.

The years marching on for Bill Halsey stamped him more and more indelibly a new kind of flag-rank officer, an aircraft carrier admiral. Meanwhile, in Europe war exploded between the Axis powers, Germany and Italy, and England and France – this in September, 1939. American sympathy was strongly with the Allies, but as in 1914 to 1917 the United States maintained official neutrality and kept the greater part of her naval power in the Atlantic to enforce it.

In the Pacific other war clouds grew steadily darker until on December 7, 1941, on what Secretary of State Hull called "a day of infamy," the Japanese made their surprise stab at Pearl Harbor.

Certain changes over twenty-five years had played their parts in bringing about a second all-oceans war.

[Chapter 8]

# The Coral Sea

WHEN GEORGE WASHINGTON retired as President in 1796 he counseled his fellow Americans always to shun "permanent alliances with any portion of the foreign world" as a means of avoiding wars with other nations. Succeeding Presidents heeded this advice, although circumstances thrust us into minor conflicts with England in 1812, Mexico in 1846, and Spain in 1898, and into a major war with Germany and Austria-Hungary in 1917.

Fortunate beyond other great powers in having so many decades of peace, Americans could thank not only George Washington's wisdom but also our geographical location. The world of the nineteenth and early twentieth centuries was in effect a larger world than we have today because travel and communication were tedious. In Washington's time an average voyage from England to America consumed forty-five days. Now the trip is made by air in a third of one day. In 1815, Andrew Jackson defeated the British at New Orleans without knowing that the treaty of peace to end hostilities had already been signed. Today Jackson would receive such news within ten minutes of its occurrence.

The very mileage across the Atlantic and Pacific Oceans helped to keep the United States out of many international quarrels. But with the laying of the Atlantic cable, and later when sailing vessels gave way to steamers, faster communication made distances seem to shrink. It became more difficult for the United States to avoid closer contacts with faraway nations.

After World War I, Americans, abhoring conflict, demanded a return to our former position of aloofness. With the election in 1920 of President Harding, isolation again became United States policy — at all costs to remain out of international troubles. This attempt to turn back the pages of history exercised great, but unforeseen, influence on the ferment that erupted into World War II.

To strengthen the cause of peace, the United States in 1921 called on the Great Powers to attend a Limitation of Armaments Conference in Washington. As a result, America and England consented to scrap certain ships of their war-swollen navies so as to meet and hold an agreed proportion of strength with other nations. By this means it was hoped to avoid costly arms rivalry and in turn to assure international tranquillity.

Between England, the United States, and Japan, the capital ships ratio agreed on in Washington and at a later conference in London was 5–5–3. This meant that for each five battleships which England and the United States maintained, Japan could have three. A similar ratio applied to vessels in other categories.

For a few years the Disarmament Treaty seemed effective; then Japan began to violate it both in spirit and in letter. She forbade foreign visitors to Pacific islands such as the Marshall group, placed in her charge by the Versailles Treaty, and set about secretly fortifying them. During the late 1920's she increased her army's strength and weaponry. Her shipyards rang with jackhammers and riveters building vessels for her fleet; and from America's West Coast she ferried hundreds of shiploads of scrap metal across the ocean to be melted and refashioned into the tools of war.

This activity, as much as could be guessed at, was reported in American newspapers. But most readers preferred to believe

Japan's repeated assurances that nothing ominous was under way. Anyhow, people reflected, at six thousand miles distance how could those funny little brown men with their gracious bows and their thick glasses be a danger to us? Congress trimmed military appropriations and trimmed them again, and almost the only protests came from professional Army and Navy people and makers of armaments. The general public had more fascinating concerns to occupy their minds, such as rampant prosperity.

The prosperity began to collapse in October, 1929. During most of the next ten years economic distress pushed farther aside bothersome thoughts about all far-off saber-rattling nations.

Franklin Roosevelt had been Assistant Secretary of the Navy during World War I. Afterward he continued his interest in military affairs, especially those of the Navy. He realized our neglect in matters of defense but when inaugurated President in 1933, could at first do little about it. His energies had to be devoted to another kind of emergency. On the day he took office every bank in the United States was closed. Thirteen million workers were out of jobs and dependent for food and shelter on public assistance, called " relief." A bushel of wheat from which to make bread was priced at less than it cost a farmer to raise, so many farmers burned their wheat in the fields. Commerce and industry were in the grip of near-paralysis. Economically, our Ship of State was hard aground.

But the next year Roosevelt began to exert his leadership on Congress and the public to restore our neglected defenses. Appropriations were driven through the House and Senate to strengthen the Army and to begin modernization of old fighting ships and construction of new. This, of course, required much time. To pass a specific appropriation could consume months, even years. To draw up plans for a modern battleship, then to prepare the detailed sixteen tons of blueprints can easily take two years, and to build her, another three or four.

Meanwhile, during the 1930's the President and many others became aware of danger signals in Europe. In Italy the warlike Benito Mussolini, " the new Caesar," made himself dictator. The Mediterranean Sea, he blustered in many a balcony speech to black-shirted Fascisti, must become, by force if necessary, " our Italian lake." Germany accepted for her master the truculent Adolf Hitler, who relieved some of the misery of his countrymen by putting them into uniform and of others by putting them to work at the booming production of " Guns – not butter! "

Half around the world, Japan's elder statesmen, moderate in their views, were driven from government office by a war party of generals, admirals, and industrialists. They built dreams about the Greater East Asia Co-Prosperity Sphere. " Japan," they proclaimed, " is on her way to her true destiny," which really meant that she intended to overrun weaker countries and to own them. While continually avowing her great love for peace Japan started her territorial expansion in 1937 with the invasion of China.

Thoughtful Americans – President Roosevelt, military strategists, observers of international affairs, and many alert citizens – felt a firming conviction that war would soon come to Europe, ignited by the dictators, and that the not-so-distant future would see an East-West struggle in the vast reaches of the Pacific. Both convictions bore evil fruit.

William Frederick Halsey, Jr., loved his profession of arms, but like so many in that profession, he hated war. He loved ships and the eternal challenge of the sea as had his father and many Halseys before him. He found fascination in dealing with men and in the fast-developing marvel of aviation. He felt pride in serving his country, which had been good to him. But he hated bloodshed and all the enormous waste of lives and wealth that is war.

For thirty-seven years he had been shaped by the United States Navy to meet a need that he and the nation hoped would never arise. Now it had arisen. Bill Halsey was ready — trained, talented, imaginative, and bold.

After the launching of the Doolittle fliers for their daring raid on Tokyo, Task Forces 16 and 18 made rapid withdrawal. Alerted by the patrol boat, a Japanese task force came racing out to search for them, and submarines were brought into the hunt. Planes from enemy carriers methodically scoured thousands of square miles of North Pacific, but hidden in a wide blanket of stormy weather, Halsey arrived safely back at Pearl Harbor a week later on April 25.

Their search fruitless, the Japanese were forced to conclude that the bombers had not, after all, come from an American carrier. Had they taken off from somewhere in the desolate Aleutians far to the north? Their intelligence service denied this. Midway Island, then, the nearest American possession, twenty-two hundred miles east of Tokyo, must have been Doolittle's starting place.

The Japanese were astonished. Not one of the bombers had come down in Japan; therefore, if they came from Midway, the flight range of the B-25 must be well above three thousand miles. This was a capability until that moment unheard of.

The enemy had long planned to seize Midway, an operation they considered preliminary to a later full-scale assault on Hawaii eleven hundred miles farther. Their ultimate goal was to establish firm bases in, from north to south, the Aleutians, Hawaii, the Gilbert, Solomon, and New Hebrides groups. These would form a jagged line several thousand miles long behind which they would operate their Co-Prosperity Sphere of Greater East Asia. Among other things, this would cut the Allied lifeline to Australia and New Zealand, which the Japanese could strangle and occupy at their pleasure.

The Doolittle raid convinced them that it was more urgent to take Midway now than they had realized. It prompted Admiral Yamamoto, a stocky, black-browed man lacking two fingers on his right hand, to action. He named the naval and air forces to be collected and the tentative date on which Midway was to be seized.

Signals flashed over the empire to the scattered ships that would make up the striking force — and with these signals, all unknowing, Yamamoto lost the coming battle.

Even before the outbreak of the war, Navy cryptographers in Washington had succeeded in solving the riddle of the Japanese military code. This was one of our most precious and best-kept secrets. At Pearl, in a heavily guarded little black building, other ingenious men of the cryptographic unit listened to Yamamoto's radioed orders and deciphered them.

They could not be certain, however, whether he intended the attack to come at the end of May or early in June, nor whether the letters "AF" that he used designated Midway alone or Oahu, largest of the Hawaiian islands. Admiral King in Washington at first believed Oahu was meant but soon came to agree with Admiral Nimitz at Pearl that Midway must be the target.

Meanwhile, far distant, the Allied command suffered a morale-jarring defeat. This was in the Java Sea, with Borneo on the north and the rich plum of Java on the south. A mixed squadron was there under the Dutch Admiral Doorman which comprised the heavy American cruiser *Houston* and the British *Exeter*, two Dutch light cruisers and one Australian, and nine destroyers. The enemy, to shield their invasion of Java, sent a three-pronged striking force of four carriers, four battleships, heavy and light cruisers, destroyers, and a number of troop transports.

Numerically, the groups were almost evenly matched.

In a desperate big-gun battle lasting seven hours the Allies lost half their ships and two more later. They managed to sink only one enemy destroyer.

Lack of enough dive bombers and fighter planes — air cover — to hit the Japanese ships and to stand off their air attacks was the principal cause of the defeat. Here was another of many bitter lessons to the Allies of the value of aircraft in modern naval warfare. A second cause was lack of a set of signals understandable to all commanders. Admiral Doorman's orders had to be translated from Dutch to English and in certain circumstances back into Dutch. The resulting delay and loss of accuracy were fatal. Java Sea was a resounding victory for the enemy.

Without pausing to consolidate their gains, the foe kept pushing on. They started around the eastern end of fifteen-hundred-mile-long New Guinea, aiming to seize the only good southeast coast harbor, Port Moresby. East of New Guinea lay the Solomons, with Tulagi Island toward their foot of chief interest. Once the Japanese could establish firm holds on Port Moresby and Tulagi, they would begin to close in control of the Coral Sea that separated New Guinea and the Solomons from Australia.

Obviously the Allies, which overwhelmingly meant the Americans, must at any cost keep open Coral Sea approaches to Australia. But they had to bring ships and supplies several thousand miles to stage their fight, whereas Japanese bases would be within a few hundred miles. Thus the enemy had every confidence that in such a battle they could annihilate our Fleet. It would knock the United States, and incidentally England, Holland, and Australia, out of the Pacific war.

In Pearl Harbor, Bill Halsey listened while Admiral Nimitz outlined these current and expected developments. The carrier *Lexington,* with protective task force, and the *Yorktown* with hers, were already hurrying south to the scene. They would need reinforcements, everything Nimitz could send. Over five feverish days the *Enterprise* and *Hornet* were restocked with fuel, ammunition, and supplies; minor, always needful repairs were rushed and new men worked into gaps in the crews. Task Force 16 put to sea, comprising the two carriers, four heavy cruisers, eight destroyers, and two tankers. Halsey was to land a squadron of Marine fighter planes on Efate in the New Hebrides, but the runway was not finished, so he placed them instead on Nouméa in New Caledonia; then he hurried on. He was still a thousand miles away when the Battle of Coral Sea was fought early in May.

Allied Intelligence had learned the broad plan of this invasion and guessed that the main Japanese effort would be directed at seizing Port Moresby. But the first action came when fighter planes from the *Yorktown* strafed and bombed troop landings on Tulagi. In spite of this, the enemy made good their occupation. Withdrawing to attend to a greater need, the *Yorktown* made rendezvous with the *Lexington.* The two task forces sped east-northeast at twenty-five knots to meet the main Japanese forces just coming around the east end of New Guinea.

Before the two fleets clashed, a tanker and her accompanying destroyer detached from the rest of our units, were sunk by planes reaching out from a Japanese carrier. The same day dive bombers from the *Yorktown* and *Lexington* caught the *Shoho,* a light carrier, with a rain of bombs that sank her. Next day, May 8, planes from the two biggest Japanese carriers traded furious air attacks with those from the American carriers. *Shokaku,* brand-new, was severely damaged. *Zuikaku* lost a large number of her first-line pilots and planes.

The *Lexington* took crippling punishment from bomb and torpedo hits. Damage-control parties augmented by a third of her crew worked valiantly to keep her in action. Just when she was believed out of danger, a motor generator left running belowdecks ignited gasoline vapors from a ruptured tank. New explosions broke out. With power lost, and listing, in early evening the mighty *Lex* had to be abandoned. An escorting destroyer drilled five torpedoes into her, and in minutes she was gone.

Neither side could claim victory in the Coral Sea, but two advantages accrued to the United States. First, we had prevented the Japanese seizure of Port Moresby and for the first time slowed their grand strategy of invasion. Second, their two biggest carriers sent limping home would take no part in the coming attack on Midway. On our side, with the *Saratoga* under repair in Washington and the *Lexington* sunk, we had only three carriers — the *Enterprise*, the *Hornet*, and the *Yorktown* — in the Pacific against at least seven still operative for the enemy.

Frustrated though Bill Halsey was at being too distant to take part in the battle, he was able to make two important contributions to our effort. First, the absence of enemy ships as he approached showed the Japanese fully occupied in parrying the *Lexington–Yorktown* forces. Second, planes from Tulagi would approach no closer to the *Enterprise* than sixty miles, which indicated that the Japanese now had radar.

From: CINCPAC
To: Task Force 16
EXPEDITE RETURN

This, Halsey knew, meant trouble was brewing elsewhere, and his guess settled on Midway. His speed back to Pearl was limited by the best speed of his tankers, and it was May 26 before the *Big E* slid to a stop beside Ford Island and let her hook down with a splash.

Bill Halsey was a sick man. Ever since his conference in California with Lieutenant Colonel Doolittle he had suffered from itching skin eruptions that spread over his whole body. Doctors called it " general dermatitis " and spoke of the combined actions of wind, salt spray, and sunshine — but privately they believed nerve strain to be the underlying cause.

For six months, with few days ashore, he had been on his bridge bearing responsibility for men and equipment. Carrier command involved occasional aircraft accidents that cost men injuries and sometimes their lives. It involved the finest mental and physical specimens of young manhood being crippled by the enemy, shot down, or lost at sea. No one of sensibility could close his mind to these tragedies or fail to die a little inside at each one. His was the constant grinding punishment that no one could share, the tremendous pressure of command.

Halsey resisted being removed from active duty. Finding himself overruled by doctors, who could put even an admiral to bed, he stalled them long enough to visit Nimitz and suggest that Admiral Ray Spruance be given his task force. Then, feverish, itching, disgusted, and snarling, " Oh, rats! " he stalked over to the hospital.

[Chapter 9]

# Midway

During Halsey's three months of inactivity the Battle of Midway took place, and two months afterward the Japanese precipitated the long, desperate struggle for Guadalcanal. Although he missed the first, it affected him by shaping the course of the war, and in the second he was actively involved.

The small group of Midway Islands were named for their location between continents. They lie close to the 180th meridian, called the International Date Line, where the westbound traveler must adjust to Asian time by advancing his calendar a full day.

There were other peculiarities. Most men never saw the island prize for which they fought. If an unknown Japanese scout plane pilot had paused for a longer look, his report to his striking force might have tipped victory to the Rising Sun. If an *Enterprise* dive bomber pilot had guessed wrong as to a direction, we would have suffered a grave defeat.

Once Admiral Nimitz knew that Yamamoto, his opposite number, was preparing to assault Midway, he set about furnishing it with every man, gun, and plane that could be spared. Beaches on the two main islands were sown with mines backed by labyrinths of barbed wire. Personnel moved about wearing steel helmets and carrying rifles, and at night, except for sentinels, all retired to caves. Eleven motor torpedo boats patrolled the lagoon and reefs, their assignment to pick up downed fliers when the battle started and to add their AA to that of ground forces; converted tuna boats and a yacht were stationed at nearby islands for rescue.

Each day patrol planes scanned a million and a half square miles of ocean for signs of the enemy. Twenty-five submarines cruised offshore in concentric circles at fifty, one hundred, and two hundred miles.

The 6th Marines under Lieutenant Colonel Shannon numbered some 2,100. Navy Captain Simard commanded fliers and service troops numbering almost 1,500. Scarcely any more men could be accommodated or more equipment made use of, except as to planes. Thirty of those on hand were old, slow patrol types. Thirty-seven more were obsolete dive bombers and fighters, including some of the " flying coffins " called Buffaloes. The others — Wildcats, Dauntless Fighters, and Vindicators — were considered to be effective — until they went up against the much faster and more maneuverable Zeroes.

Defensively, the Midway commanders felt secure from invasion by muscular brown men leaping off barges into the surf to wade ashore. These could be dealt with. It would be another story if numerous enemy ships stood miles at sea under a protective umbrella of planes while their big guns hurled high explosive to blast the islands to rubble. It would take scores of planes, and better ones than the islands had, to chase the Japanese battlewagons away.

Admiral Nimitz assembled every available combat ship for the coming test. Halsey's old Task Force 16 now consisted of the carriers *Enterprise* and *Hornet,* six cruisers, and nine destroyers. TF 17 was the carrier *Yorktown,* two cruisers, and five destroyers. Rear Admiral Fletcher, overall commander, had his flag on the *Yorktown.*

Our two task forces held rendezvous three hundred fifty miles east of Midway on June 2. Fletcher messaged his fleet, " Enemy attacked Dutch Harbor this morning." This action in the far-off Aleutians obviously was meant to divert American attention, but for the time being was ignored.

The Japanese approached in three forces. From the southwest came their occupation force, three thousand troops on transports guarded by twenty-nine destroyers, two battleships, a light aircraft carrier, and eight cruisers. From the northwest a carrier striking force, hidden for many hours behind a weather front, comprised four aircraft carriers, two battleships, three cruisers, sixteen destroyers, and supply ships. Commanding was Admiral Nagumo who, aboard the same *Akagi*, had led the attack on Pearl Harbor. The third group approached from the west. It was commanded by Isoroku Yamamoto himself, comprising seven battleships, a light carrier, three cruisers, thirteen destroyers, and four supply ships. His flagship, the brand-new *Yamoto,* was over sixty-three thousand tons, almost twenty-thousand more than our first of the *Iowa* class commissioned a year later. The *Yamoto* was the world's most formidable fighting ship.

The Japanese were throwing their greatest strength into this operation. Although the relative naval lineups were then unknown to each side, combat ships other than submarines stood at:

| JAPANESE | | AMERICAN |
|---|---|---|
| 11 | *battleships* | 0 |
| 6 | *carriers* | 3 |
| 14 | *cruisers* | 8 |
| 58 | *destroyers* | 14 |
| 89 | | 25 |

Nimitz had warned, "Balsa (code for Midway) air force must inflict prompt and early damage to Jap carrier flight decks." Admiral Bellinger as Commander, Patrol Wings Hawaiian Area, got down to specifics with the estimate that Japanese carriers would approach Midway at twenty-seven knots and would launch planes no farther out than two hundred miles. "Catalinas taking off Midway at dawn and flying seven hundred miles at one hundred knots each can scan an 8-degree sector. To scan 180 degrees, twenty-three planes will be needed."

Fast, accurate reports of enemy positions and numbers were vital. Because Midway had not enough Catalinas for patrol the Army 431st Bombardment Squadron on Oahu sent a dozen Flying Fortresses. While both types fanned out on search, Midway stayed on alert.

The islands' defense could not spare men for plane maintenance, which meant that after flying fifteen-hour patrols the crews must spend more hours making repairs. And because somebody had accidentally tripped demolition charges under the aviation gasoline tanks, all refueling had to be done by hand from fifty-five gallon cans.

The unknown Japanese plan called for a three-day air attack from carriers, then a big-gun bombardment. When rats were the only life remaining on Midway, troops would be put ashore.

On June 3 scout planes sighted a few enemy ships, could not make certain of types and numbers before losing them, suspected a more important force behind that northwest weather front, and at the most inconvenient moments were forced to turn back because of diminishing fuel.

But what they did find, they attacked. Nine Fortresses came out to hit the occupation force of "five battleships or heavy cruisers and about forty others." Because of extra gas tanks, each Fortress could carry only four six-hundred-pound bombs. They damaged a cruiser and a transport. Four Catalina crews with no bombing experience managed to attach aerial torpedoes to their planes and lugged them out to sea at night. They charged up the moonpath to silhouette their targets and blew a hole in the tanker *Akebono Maru*. On the long flight home they learned at dawn that Midway was under attack.

From three in the morning of June 4 all defending fighter, dive bomber, and torpedo plane personnel were assembled and eager to take off. For half their number, this was their last day.

Catalinas flew off in search of Nagumo's carriers while Fortresses went to look again for the occupation force. At 0525 a Catalina flashed: "UNIDENTIFIED PLANES, BEARING 320, DISTANCE 100 MILES." Minutes later: "ENEMY CARRIERS 150 MILES, 330 DEGREES." Presently a local radar notified: "MANY PLANES APPROACHING, 89 MILES, 320 DEGREES."

Every plane on Midway except one noncombat utility took to the air. The experience of all, to a greater or lesser extent, was like that of Major Parks's flight of Buffaloes and Wildcats. They spied an oncoming mass of Zeroes below, and dived at them. Immediately they found themselves outgunned, outnumbered, and far outclassed.

The Zeroes literally chewed up the slower, less maneuverable American planes. They flew circles around them. One moment above, next moment they were below. They set planes afire, shot others down. They machine-gunned and killed two pilots dangling in the sky from parachutes. The only chance of escape was to plunge at full power for the cover of ground fire . . . but some pilots were unable to pull out in time.

Enemy carrier dive bombers, some carrying bombs that weighed seventeen hundred pounds, lambasted the two main islands. Confident that these blows were shattering all defense, Pilot Lieutenant Tomonaga radioed Admiral Nagumo aboard the *Akagi*, "No need for second attack." Actually, Midway was still very much in the battle in spite of oil tanks and seaplane hangars afire, the dispensary roof with a large red cross painted on it sailing high into the air, and the powerhouse and galley gone. When the post exchange blew apart, a hurtling can of beer knocked the wind out of a machine gunner.

While combat raged on and above Midway an even greater battle had burst out at sea.

On that morning of June 4 when the messages of the Midway scout plane had been received by Rear Admiral Fletcher's task forces, *Enterprise* threw up fifty-seven fighters, dive bombers, and torpedo planes, and *Hornet*'s air groups of similar size were also aloft heading for the enemy a hundred fifty miles away.

Now began the complicated advancing, turning, evasion, and milling tactics of more than one hundred warships and a dozen and a half tankers and transports scattered over half the compass. The main bout was a slugging match between carriers.

Of the *Hornet's* six squadrons launched, Torpedo 8, fifteen Devastators, for some reason did not pause to rendezvous with the others but " lit a shuck " for the horizon alone. Lieutenant Commander Waldron outdistanced his own fighter escort and was trying to get at the *Haruna* and *Kirishima* when the Zeroes fell on him. Planes that survived their hail of bullets ran on into walls of AA fire that smashed instruments, cut control cables, tore holes in wings, and killed pilots and gunners. Fourteen Devastators plunged burning into the sea.

Ensign Gay, the only man of thirty in the flight to survive, was hit twice in the left arm. He pulled one bullet out with his teeth and managed to hold his plane on straight course the long two minutes necessary for torpedo aim. He let go at the *Kaga,* then swept past her bridge. " I could see the little Jap captain jumping up and down." A shell blasted his controls, wounded his foot, and sent him crashing into the sea. Gay wiggled free of the wreck, struggling in the wash of racing enemy ships. Swimming slowly and holding a deflated rubber life raft over his head, he escaped notice.

*Enterprise's* Torpedo 6 roared at the *Akagi*. During their sustained run to launch torpedoes, Zeroes came at them with machine guns blazing and knocked down ten. The others were forced to veer away without launching.

The *Yorktown* got off thirty-five planes, six of them Wildcat fighters. They stayed close to the torpedo bearers and were joined by ten wandering *Enterprise* fighters. While the group sped the dozen miles toward target they were pounded by twice as many Zeroes. Three Wildcats dived flaming into the ocean. One torpedo plane just starting his run at the *Akagi* blew apart. Five made their drops, then three of these were shot down.

Thirty-five American torpedo planes out of forty-one had been lost. Not one torpedo caused serious damage. But while every Zero in the sky worked over these planes and every ship's AA guns flung lead at them, our dive bombers had better success with the *Kaga,* the *Akagi,* and the *Soryu.*

Leader of thirty-three *Enterprise* Dauntlesses was Lieutenant Commander McClusky who at Kwajalein had almost splashed a Zero on the carrier's deck. Again on the warpath, McClusky was searching for the enemy's main striking force. Mounting to twenty thousand feet, in the cloudless sky he could scan ninety-five thousand square miles of ocean. Except for tiny Midway a hundred miles southeast, it was all blank.

He flew on another seventy-five miles, needing to find the enemy carriers before they could launch a strike against our own. Miles behind him, the *Hornet*'s group, also searching, sent twenty-two bombers home for lack of fuel and pressed on another half hour with thirteen Dauntlesses and ten Wildcats. Trying southeast, then northeast, these planes dallied too long. Before they could run back to Midway the Wildcat engines gasped and ceased ticking over. Ten pilots ditched, of whom eight survived. Two of the Dauntlesses managed to splash in Midway lagoon and their crews waded ashore.

McClusky, still searching, reasoned that the enemy might have reversed their southeast course. He veered his bombers northwest. This, Captain Murray of the *Enterprise* declared, was the most important decision of the entire battle. Twenty minutes passed. Twenty-five. Half the fuel of the bomber group was gone. About to give up and turn back, McClusky noticed a faint white feather in the sea. Was that a destroyer's wake? Two minutes closer, far to the north, he spied three carriers escorted by great battlewagons – the *Soryu* leading, *Kaga* to the west, *Akagi* to the east. Unseen behind clouds the *Hiryu* brought up the rear.

McClusky's glance around the sky showed no Zeroes in sight. He ordered half his bombers to go after the *Akagi* and the rest at the *Kaga.* The big Rising Sun painted on their yellow decks made perfect bull's eyes to aim at.

On the *Kaga* thirty planes stood ready for takeoff, with thirty more armed and fueled waiting on her hangar deck. Suddenly four bombs rained down. They smashed her bridge, wiping out every man on it, the captain included. Explosions skittered from plane to plane the length of both flight and hangar decks. A pillar of fire leaped almost a third of a mile into the air and a smoke shroud, slashed by tonguing flames, hugged the entire ship. Her helmsman dead, she lurched off on a drunken course.

The *Soryu,* also with sixty planes ready to fly, took three direct hits. On both top decks spattering gasoline started fires that raced hungrily fore and aft. A magazine blew up. Her engines stopped. Through a megaphone Captain Yanagimoto shouted down from his bridge: " Abandon ship! Abandon ship. *Banzai!* " A rising fence of flames erased him from view. Some of the crew were trapped belowdecks, but all who could rushed for the safety of the bow. An explosion blew them into the sea.

While this was in progress, *Yorktown*'s Bombing 3 was working over Nagumo's *Akagi.* She had forty planes aboard, the rest of her quota still away pounding Midway. Her front fighters tried to take off, but two bombs split the flight deck amidships and aft. At first the damage appeared surmountable, but her stern pumps were broken. Flames from a burning fighter plane climbed her bridge. The fire spread. Hurriedly, Admiral Nagumo slid down a rope overside to a destroyer and his staff transferred to a cruiser. The *Akagi,* her decks ablaze from bow to stern, lay dead in the water.

Of McClusky's Dauntless pilots, eighteen were lost, some of them from running out of fuel. What remained of Bombing 3 winged back to the *Yorktown* only to be waved off because her radar had picked up a coming strike. And it came: nine fighters

Admiral William F. Halsey in July, 1945.

U.S.S. *Enterprise* in April, 1944.

Japanese torpedo bomber going down in flames astern U.S.S. *Washington* after attacking our light carrier *Essex*. This was during the Third Fleet raid on Formosa (Taiwan).

Two views of B–25's taking off from flight deck of carrier *Hornet* to raid Tokyo on April 18, 1942.

Admiral Halsey being piped aboard the carrier *Saratoga.*

Admiral William F. Halsey, COMSOPAC, and Major General Alexander Vandergrift confer at Halsey's Nouméa headquarters.

Japanese " Zeke " attacked by Navy plane. Photo was taken by gun camera installed in leading edge of plane wing.

Admiral Halsey, COMSOPAC, on inspection tour on Vella Lavella Island, Solomons.

Fire fighters battle flames on *Saratoga's* flight deck off Iwo Jima, February 21, 1945.

Thanksgiving dinner aboard battleship *New Jersey* in 1944.

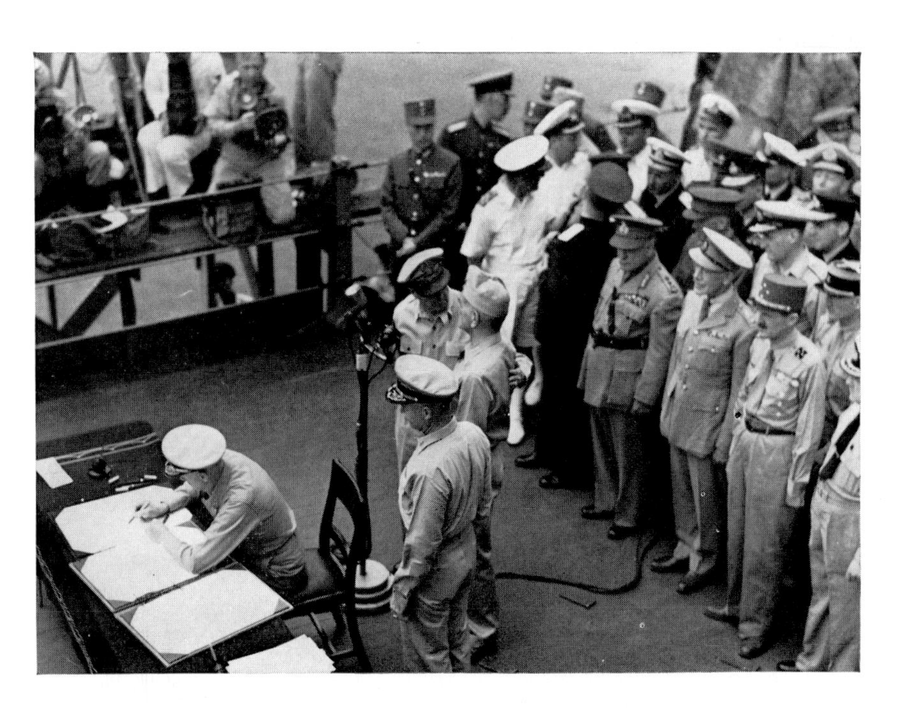

Historic surrender ceremony aboard battleship *Missouri* in Tokyo Bay, 1945. Admiral Nimitz signs the surrender document in presence of General MacArthur, Admiral Halsey, and Allied representatives.

Admiral Halsey wearing the four stars of a full admiral.

and eighteen Japanese bombers from the fourth big enemy carrier, *Hiryu*. Combat air patrol flew to intercept, and shot down ten bombers. But there were many more. Three bombs scored and one knifed down three decks before it exploded. The blast snuffed out fires in two boilers and filled the engine rooms with fumes. Steam pressure died. The *Yorktown* lost way.

Quickly, Admiral Fletcher inspected the flight and hangar decks, then discovered he could not get back to his flag bridge because of dense smoke. To renew communications with his task force, he and his staff hastened like monkeys down a line to the cruiser *Astoria*. While damage control parties fought fires and the engineers got the *Yorktown*'s boilers going and built up her speed to twenty knots, Admiral Spruance had sent two cruisers and two destroyers to serve as AA reinforcements. But in the afternoon Japanese torpedo planes came over and four managed effective drops on the carrier before being shot down. When two torpedoes blasted her at almost the same spot port-amidships, "she seemed to leap out of the water."

Control lost, she drifted in a dazed circle. Wounded were taken off, then her crew abandoned her. Hundreds gazed back from the decks of departing rescue ships as in the golden sunset *Yorktown* drifted, listing, mourned by a lone destroyer.

One of her orphaned scout planes reported an enemy carrier with two battleships, three cruisers, and four destroyers a hundred sixty miles west of the *Enterprise*. They were headed north. The *Big E* threw twenty-four Dauntlesses into the air, some of them refugees from the *Yorktown*. In an hour they sighted columns of smoke from the *Kaga, Akagi*, and *Soryu*. Farther on they found the fleeing *Hiryu* and friends. Starting their dives at nineteen thousand feet, the bombers laid four big eggs on the *Hiryu*'s deck and three more close astern. Instantly, flames enveloped the entire ship. Knowing she was finished, the last dive bombers in line swerved to attack a battleship and a cruiser.

The *Soryu* was the first Japanese carrier to sink, helped by three torpedoes from the U.S. submarine *Nautilus.* Fifteen miles away, Ensign Gay, still afloat under his trusty life raft, watched the *Kaga* burning. Several hundred of her crew still waited to be taken off when a Japanese cruiser fired point-blank at her waterline, and she went down. The *Akagi* and *Hiryu* sank the next morning, June 5.

In the last battle action the morning of June 5, Fortresses bombed " a cruiser that sank in fifteen seconds." She proved to be our submarine *Grayling* instead, however, which had only crash-dived.

Ensign Gay, picked up that afternoon, was in fair condition. Asked what he had done for his wounds he said, " I just soaked them in salt water." Fifty other men were picked up, thirty-five of them from the *Hiryu.*

Although listing at forty degrees, the *Yorktown* was still afloat. A working party went aboard and a mine sweeper took her in tow. The destroyer *Hammann,* lashed to her starboard side, supplied power and pumped water to fight her numerous fires. Suddenly a lookout spied four oncoming torpedo wakes. One torpedo went astern, one hit the *Hammann* broadside, and the other two struck the *Yorktown.* As the *Hammann* sank, her depth charges exploded, killing most of her crew. The *Yorktown,* Captain Buckmaster knew, now was doomed. Hastily an officer telephoned various working parties below, " Abandon ship! "

A group on the fourth deck found themselves trapped by sprung safety doors. Shocked, the officer on the bridge could scarcely find his voice.

" Do you men realize the trouble you're in? "

" Sure." There was a pause. " We've got an acey-deucy game going." A longer pause. " When you slam the torpedoes into her, put 'em right where we are. Understand? We want this to be quick."

Needing no torpedoes, the *Yorktown* turned over and went to her rest in three thousand fathoms on June 6.

Score of the battle in losses:

| Japan | | United States |
|---|---|---|
| 3,500 | *men* | 307 |
| 253 | *planes* | 150 |
| 4 | *carriers* | 1 |
| 1 | *cruisers* | 0 |
| 0 | *destroyers* | 1 |

Six months after Pearl Harbor naval power in the Pacific had been put back into balance. The Battle of Midway was a decisive victory for the United States.

Japan's threat to Hawaii and to our West Coast was ended. Her expansion into the Far East had to be curtailed and her progress southward changed from aggression to holding. Although she never fully made up for the loss of four aircraft carriers, there was a lot of World War II remaining to be fought.

[Chapter 10]

# COMSOPAC

At Pearl Harbor in mid-September, 1942, Admiral Nimitz took a friend with him aboard the *Saratoga* where he was to present decorations to a number of sailors and Marines. When the crew were lined up on the flight deck, Nimitz announced on the public-address system, "Men, I have a surprise for you. Bill Halsey is back."

The cheers that responded and the shower of caps in the air left Halsey with eyes glistening.

During a wait for his new command to be assembled, a task force with the *Enterprise* again as his flagship, Halsey went on an airplane tour of the South Pacific. He wanted to familiarize himself with our island outposts and the many more held by the enemy, and to confer with Allied leaders in New Zealand and with General Douglas MacArthur in Australia.

CINCPAC was the symbol of Admiral Nimitz's command of all Allied naval forces in the Pacific. COMSOPAC designated the South Pacific, headed by Vice Admiral Ghormley. SOWES–PAC, under Army control, was General MacArthur. During the months of Halsey's inactivity, our situation in the last two areas had steadily worsened.

When the Japanese attempt to turn the corner of New Guinea had been blunted at the Battle of Coral Sea, their strategists set about winning the huge island and particularly its prize, Port Moresby, by land. For this purpose they put troops ashore on

Guinea's easily controlled north coast. Australians pinned them down there and held despite scant fighter plane support and a supply line so long that every bullet and K ration had to be flown by bomber from Australia.

When five thousand Japanese reinforcements arrived, the Aussies grudgingly fell back. Over several months they retreated through some of the world's most difficult country to stay alive in, let alone to fight in. In the steamy, malarial jungles mosquitoes were so big, the Aussies said wryly, that "machine gunners mistake them for Zeroes." Disputing every mile, they retreated up the seven-thousand-foot high Owen Stanley mountains, then down their south slopes into more New Guinea jungle.

General MacArthur was determined at all costs to hold Port Moresby. It would be the base from which, eventually, he intended to fight his way back to the Philippines. Only thirty-two miles from Port Moresby the tough Australians at last managed to stop the Japanese advance.

East of New Guinea the Solomon archipelago begins five degrees below the equator. Extending several hundred miles, the islands lie northwest-southeast in two parallel groups, and the wide channel between them, New Georgia Sound, came to be known as "the Slot." The Japanese were already firmly planted on Tulagi, Rabaul, and other islands and in July they landed on Guadalcanal and set about building an airfield. Once it was operative, their planes could fan out hundreds of miles to cut all Allied supply lines to New Zealand, to Australia, and northeast to Hawaii and the United States.

The great threat of this move could not go unchallenged. Our Navy rushed the First and Fifth Marine Divisions up from New Zealand. Escort warships poured a heavy bombardment on Guadalcanal to soften shore resistance; then the Marines climbed over the rails of their transports and down cargo nets into Higgins boats. Like dozens of water bugs, these boats chugged in to ground in the surf and the Marines waded onto the wide beach. The Japanese strategy was to give way for the present, and we gained their airfield three miles inland, which we named Henderson. Field guns, trucks, bulldozers, and small mountains of supplies were still being assembled on the beach when counterattacking Japanese bombing planes and fighters roared down from Rabaul. Fiercely they strafed our vessels standing offshore, but had they instead concentrated on the easier task of destroying our supplies on shore, in one hour the Marines would have been without food, water, or ammunition.

But the Japanese were not finished with these invaders. Next day our air reconnaissance reported a strong enemy naval force entering the Slot northwest of Guadalcanal. To shield our still-unloading transports, two cruiser and destroyer groups of Australian and American ships took positions on either side of Savo Island. In spite of this ambush, that night, August 9, they, not the Japanese, were taken by surprise by a cruiser force at almost point-blank range.

With some of our ships silhouetted against the distant burning transport, enemy aim was deadly. In thirteen minutes we lost the heavy cruisers *Astoria, Quincy,* and *Vincennes,* and the Aussie *Canberra* sunk or sinking, with the *Chicago* badly damaged.

It was Japan's most brilliant naval victory and proof of their mastery of the area in the air and on the sea.

Strangely, their task force did not continue southeast to annihilate our all but undefended transports. It was one of several instances during the war when the enemy showed rare talent for missing an opportunity. Instead, they wheeled about and headed away. So, in a feverish hurry, did our transports, although some were still only half unloaded – leaving the Marines ashore very much on their own.

Now for the men on Guadalcanal began many agonizing weeks. Our fighter, bombing, and cargo planes, regularly outnumbered, managed to deliver only a trickle of supplies. The occasional handfuls of fighters we managed to put down on

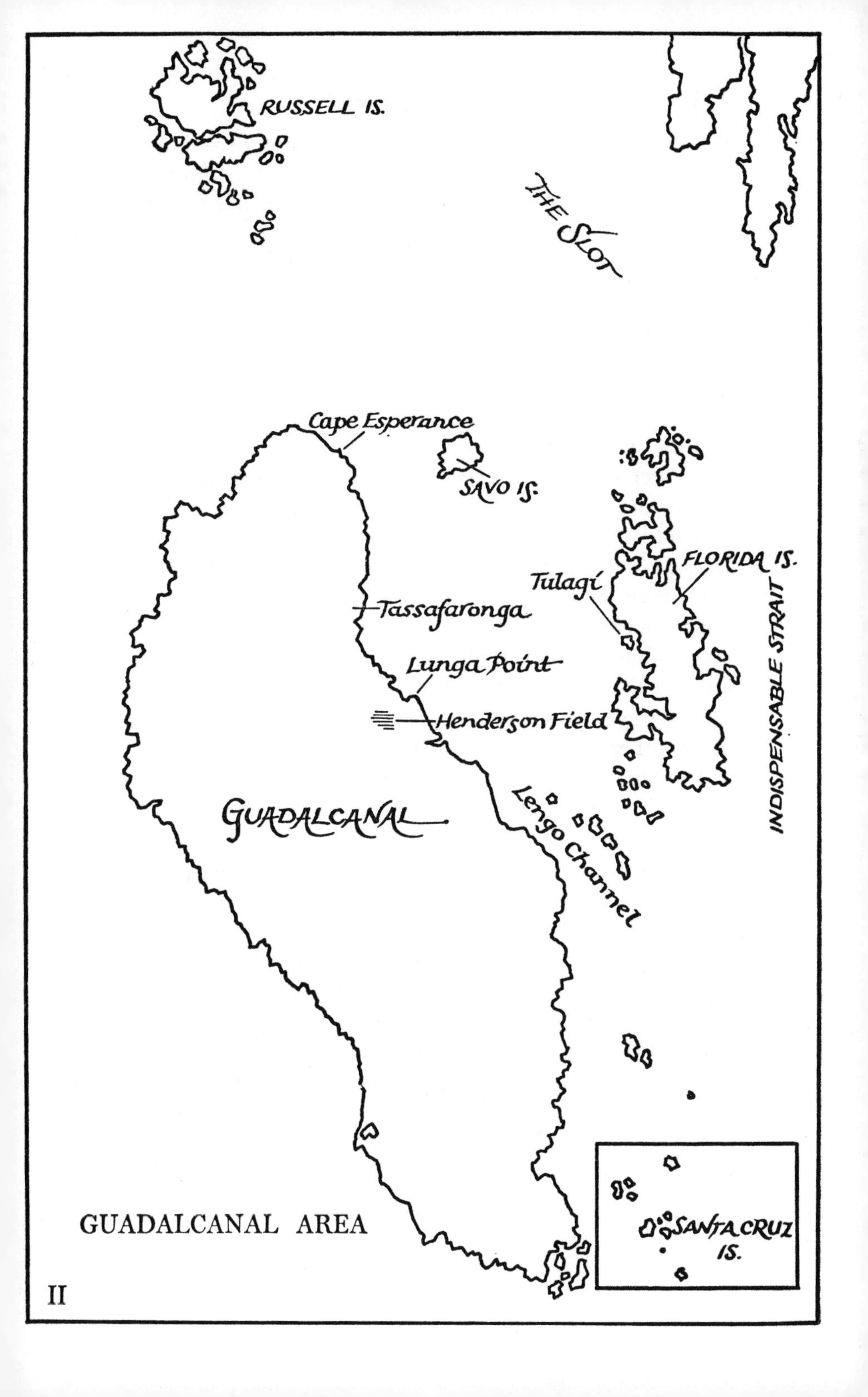


GUADALCANAL AREA

Henderson Field were subject to constant dive bomber attacks. With Japanese fleet units constantly prowling the Slot, we had not enough naval strength to smash our way through with reinforcements. Ashore, Japanese troops outnumbering ours three to one kept up around-the-clock attacks.

But the Marines held. With the tenacity traditional of their service through all United States history, the "dogfaces" dug in and held.

Heat and humidity in the Solomons are constant and debilitating to men's bodies and minds. Except for Henderson Field and the beaches, all is jungle, crowding hardwood trees a hundred feet tall and six feet in diameter. Their branches and trunks are festooned with vines, creepers, and man-high ferns. It is dark in the jungle, impenetrable for more than a few feet. Insect life abounds: three-inch wasps, scorpions, enormous spiders, some of them poisonous, ants whose bite feels like the burn of a cigarette end. Leeches drop unnoticed from trees onto passers-by and suck their blood. There are lizards three feet long, snakes of the constrictor type, and crocodiles. Malaria, dengue fever, dysentery, "jungle rot," prey on humans, plus a dozen other diseases for which cures are unknown.

The Japanese, experienced in jungle fighting as our men were not, had every advantage. To supply and reinforce their troops was by comparison not difficult. Every appearance of their "Louie the Louse," a carrier-based spotter plane, meant ship bombardment was about to resume, with Louie dropping flares or radioing target corrections. Cruisers' twelve-inch guns occasionally were augmented by fourteen-inch high-explosive shells from battleships. Helpless to reply, the Marines could only crouch in foxholes, their faces in their hands while they endured the earth-jarring shocks.

Nights, "Washing Machine Charlie," named for his loose-sounding twin engines, cruised overhead, dropping an occasional bomb to make sleep impossible and nerves ragged. Raids and skirmishes were constant at various jungle points along the perimeter of the airfield. The wounded and sick multiplied. Over the weeks few men failed to become feverish from malaria.

In these conditions there was little to go on but hope. " Don't worry, buddy. Any day now Uncle Sam will send in plenty of reinforcements." But the few that could be delivered through Japanese superior power were offset by losses. Men began to question, " Why doesn't the Navy bring up carriers and knock the Nips out of the sky? "

" Why doesn't the Navy chase those Jap battlewagons out of the Slot? "

And, as morale sagged, " Where *is* our Navy? "

Island-hopping in a four-engine Coronado, Bill Halsey, with two aides and two rear admirals, planned to stop on Guadalcanal. However, a CINCPAC dispatch caught up with him: " Proceed Suva and Nouméa," which meant the visit was considered needlessly hazardous. Next day, October 18, as the seaplane's engines died in the harbor of Nouméa several hundred miles south in the New Caledonia group, a whaleboat put out. Vice Admiral Ghormley's flag lieutenant came aboard, saluted and handed Halsey an envelope marked SECRET.

From: CINCPAC
To: W. F. Halsey, admiral

YOU WILL TAKE COMMAND OF THE SOUTH PACIFIC AREA AND SOUTH PACIFIC FORCES IMMEDIATELY

Frowning, Halsey reread it. Yes, it said what he thought. He passed it to his aides.

Standing there in the big Coronado, he felt stunned. COMINCH Admiral King had given no hint of this assignment when they had talked last month in Washington. There had been no mention of it by Admiral Nimitz. Suddenly, Bill Halsey was responsible for our entire war effort in several hundred thousand square miles of South Pacific.

He had never had experience campaigning with the Army and now must also direct Australian, New Zealand, and Free French forces. Not yet had Halsey gained a clear mental picture of the Allies' situation and scattered strength. He knew the Japanese were still thrusting southward, occupying one key island after another. New Zealand was alarmed and wanted the regiments she had contributed to the European war rushed home from North Africa. Australia wanted hers home too; meanwhile, she was hurriedly building the Brisbane Line for a last stand halfway down that continent.

Bill Halsey growled some comments under his breath. Then he threw his shoulders back. "Get me ashore," he barked to his aides. During the short whaleboat ride he was silent, his heavy jaw pushed out, narrowed eyes fixed on something no other person could see. When taken by surprise, that was his way: first the growls, then some vigorous reaction, then silence while his determination began to temper itself like steel.

Greeted by his longtime friend Admiral Ghormley, he was taken to COMSOPAC headquarters aboard the repair ship *Argonne*. The men conferred two hours and had a meal together. Later Halsey formally relieved Ghormley. He watched him go out in the whaleboat to the Coronado, watched it skim over the water and lift into the air. As the seaplane vanished into the northeast Bill Halsey stalked back to his headquarters and called a staff meeting.

After our heavy losses off Savo Island the United States held our only three carriers in the Pacific out of the combat zone, unwilling to risk them unless the enemy committed sufficiently important fleet elements. Late in August a Japanese four-transport occupation force headed down the Slot, and a hundred miles away, followed with a striking force of five carriers with battleships, cruisers, and destroyers. This challenge was accepted. The *Enterprise* and *Saratoga* went after the striking force, but the *Wasp*, a victim of garbled intelligence, withdrew south. In the battle we sank the carrier *Ryujo* and a transport, and shot down ninety-one planes. We lost twenty planes, and the *Enterprise* took three direct hits that killed seventy men. She had to go limping off for Pearl. Both sides withdrew.

Soon the *Hornet's* arrival put our carrier strength back at three. This lasted two days. A Japanese submarine's torpedo blasted the *Saratoga,* but she kept afloat and went creeping away for Pearl. Then the *Wasp* was sunk and two hundred men lost with her. Now we were down to one aircraft carrier in the entire Pacific.

A group of our transports, despite losing two, managed to land the Seventh Marine Regiment, part of the First Division, on Guadalcanal. Early in October elements of the Americal Division were brought up from Nouméa closely guarded by a task force against the "Tokyo Express," nightly raiders from the northern Solomons. Off Cape Esperance the two forces almost repeated the Battle of Savo except that this time the Americans surprised the Japanese. Again the result was not a knockout. We landed our Americal Division but the enemy landed two of theirs.

The day Bill Halsey became COMSOPAC, October 18, only one dive bomber was operational at Henderson Field. Daily, mechanics cannibalized wrecked planes in order to put others into the air, and daily, bomb holes had to be filled in the runways. Occasional fighters, dive bombers, and B-17's in fours and sixes slipped past Japanese air patrols and came in to land. Their pilots were constantly on call, some becoming so exhausted that they crawled under the wings of their craft and beat the ground in sheer hysteria. Air attacks and shellings and two- and three-pronged Japanese infantry drives occurred every day. Trucks operated sluggishly on low-octane captured gasoline, and the men were glad to eat captured rice. Even brackish water was rationed.

When cargo ships dashed inshore and attempted to land supplies, it brought an immediate Condition Red (air alert). They had to pull up their anchors and go zigzagging away. During one thirty-six-hour period the battleships *Kongo* and *Haruna* stood in the Slot and pitched a thousand fourteen-inch shells at Henderson Field. Facedown in their foxholes, the defenders began to wonder if they had been abandoned by the outside world.

The question occupied every mind, *Where is the Navy?*

Just before sunset of another dismally humid day Major General Vandegrift of the Marines sat listlessly in his tent. Someone thrust a radio message in his hand. He read it and with a yell leaped into the air.

Two aides shrank away. One whispered, "The Old Man's cracking up!"

"General, what is it?" the other ventured. "What's gone wrong?"

"Wrong?" Vandegrift flourished the message. "Bill Halsey's been made COMSOPAC. Now we'll get back in the war!"

In an hour the news was known to every defender. Marines argued whether Halsey was worth two battleships or three. They concluded his value was "a couple of aircraft carriers." Their resistance to a raid that night was so spirited that a Japanese prisoner wondered if the Americans had somehow landed another regiment.

Two evenings later Halsey was consulting in his quarters aboard the *Argonne* with Generals Vandegrift, Patch, Harmon, Holcomb, and Vogel. No discussion was needed whether to attempt to keep our foothold on Guadalcanal; the question was "How?" Vandegrift and Harmon, fresh from the scene, consumed two hours detailing their desperate situation.

"Can you hang on?" Halsey asked.

"I can," Vandegrift said, "if I get a lot more support."

Admiral Turner, commanding Amphibious Forces Pacific, explained that almost every day available transports were becoming fewer, not only from combat losses but also from breakdowns that resulted from long-delayed engine and hull repairs.

Guadalcanal had no sheltered base for unloading men and supplies, not enough open water for evasion under attack, and enemy submarines were plentiful. To make matters worse, there were not enough warships to give the transports adequate protection. If the men on Guadalcanal wondered, Where is the Navy? the answer, Turner summed up, was that the Navy was straining every nerve " but we just haven't got enough nerves."

Vandegrift made no comment. He looked at Bill Halsey rigid in his chair, eyes slitted, his bulldog jaw thrust out.

" Go on back there," Halsey told him. " I'll send you every man and gun that I can."

The conference ended.

Although information was difficult to obtain as to the immediate moves of the Japanese, their broad strategy remained obvious. They wanted Henderson Field for a base from which their land bombers could support a showdown assault on our fleet. Once they crushed it, they could at leisure mop up Port Moresby and our few island outposts, wall off New Zealand and Australia, and be undisputed masters of the South Pacific.

But they faced irksome delay so long as our Marine and Army units clung to Henderson Field. Such delay gave the Allies time to gain strength. To end it the Japanese stepped up their pressure on Guadalcanal – and the inevitable battle hurried nearer.

Nightly the enemy landed reinforcements in numbers that soon would become overwhelming. Nightly they brought more planes, more submarines, more surface vessels to grind up our thin flow of men and supplies. Meanwhile, to the northeast they assembled a powerful fleet. Our Intelligence counted four aircraft carriers, four battleships, and forty cruisers and destroyers, plus numerous troop transports and various fuel and supply ships.

Halsey counted and recounted his insufficient armor. He had the Third Fleet, made up of two meager task forces. The first was the remnant of our Cape Esperance action, the old battleship *Washington,* one heavy and one light cruiser and three destroyers. The second, commanded by Admiral Murray, former captain of the *Enterprise* under Halsey, had the carrier *Hornet,* two heavy and two light cruisers, and six destroyers.

Beyond that he had one ardent hope. Another task force was en route at top speed from Pearl Harbor three thousand miles away. Led by the hastily repaired *Enterprise,* it comprised one battleship, a heavy and a light cruiser, and eight destroyers. But Halsey knew Admiral Kinkaid, commanding, could not arrive by October 23. That was the date Intelligence said the Japanese were going to attack.

The tense procession of hours on the twenty-third inched past. No attack. The enemy fleet were delaying, every hour expecting word that Henderson Field had fallen. It hadn't; our troops there still doggedly hung on, literally buying time with their blood. Could the brave men who paid the highest price have known it, their sacrifice was not in vain. For at 1245 hours on the twenty-fourth, northeast of the New Hebrides, the *Enterprise* brought her task force steaming over the horizon to combine with the waiting task force of the *Hornet.*

Now we had two carriers – two against four held by the Japanese. But two carriers, Bill Halsey knew, tactically can be four times as effective as one. Before the *Big E*'s arrival there had been no hope for success. Now we had a fighting chance.

[Chapter 11]

# Carrier Duel

THE STAGE was set over hundreds of square miles. In the wings we had eighty-five fighters and heavy bombers assembled on Espiritu Santo. The actors took their positions ready for the raising of the curtain and the beginning of the performance.

In place of the overture, enemy planes made new attacks on Henderson Field, and American bombers on a long flight from General MacArthur's SOWESPAC overflew Guadalcanal northward to strike at enemy shipping concentrated at Rabaul and air bases on the same island, New Britain. Like ushers patrolling the aisles, submarines of both sides roved the Solomon Sea.

Halsey held his naval power east of both the northern and southern tips of Guadalcanal. Off Savo Island opposite the northern tip, Admiral Scott commanded our smallest force, the battleship *Washington,* two cruisers, and three destroyers. Some two hundred and fifty miles away toward the Santa Cruz Islands the combined *Enterprise* and *Hornet* task force waited out of reach of land-based bombers but ready to surge at the Japanese flank.

In the rainy dawn of the twenty-fifth an enemy cruiser and four destroyers landed troops on Guadalcanal. It was noon before the sun dried Henderson Field enough for dive bombers to take off to dispute the landing. Joined by six Espiritu B-17's, they damaged the cruiser and one destroyer. Meanwhile, our ranging patrols sighted two enemy forces advancing from the north, but promptly lost them. Halsey sent *Enterprise* patrols on an evening search and ordered Admiral Scott to make a night sweep around Savo. Neither found the enemy.

From twelve thousand feet early the next morning the *Big E*'s scouts sighted a massive collection of Japanese ships steaming toward Guadalcanal. These were the two forces glimpsed yesterday, now combined. As they were already south of Savo, Scott remained on station there to await a possible following force. The enemy numbered four aircraft carriers, four battleships, nine cruisers, and twenty-six destroyers.

Halsey's final dispatch to all combat commands had three ringing words:

ATTACK REPEAT ATTACK

Now on the COMSOPAC headquarters ship *Argonne* at Nouméa began for Bill Halsey long hours of tension. His part in the battle was largely over, though it had not yet been fought. Responsibility for the outcome was his. War is not a series of games in which one lost today can be offset with a victory tomorrow; in war each battle may alter the fate of nations. Single battles frequently have.

He paced the deck of the *Argonne,* chin sunk on chest, hands clasped behind him. His aides, striving not to watch, hovered within call. Wheeling, he stalked to the communications center and paused in its doorway. No message was handed to him. As yet there was no news.

He resumed his moody pacing. For the fiftieth time Halsey went over in his mind the strength of the enemy and their last-known position. What about unknown strength – how much was there of that? Then the placement of his own units: had he made the best possible use of his strongest ones? Was he depending too much on weaker ones? Was he, anywhere, wasting strength, the correct use of which might tip the scales to victory?

Beckoning to a steward for coffee, he stood at the rail sipping it and gazing over jungle-carpeted Nouméa. With all his heart Halsey wished himself on the flag bridge of his old *Enterprise*. There, with the crackle of AA in his ears and the steel-helmet-pounding smash of five-inch guns, watching Wildcat fighters whip off the deck to meet oncoming Zeroes, action filled a man's thoughts. He had no time for anxiety.

Suppose he had overlooked some one crucial thing? The United States could be virtually ruled off the sixty-four million square miles of Pacific, along with her allies, the British, the Australians, the New Zealanders, and the valiant handful of Free French. This could be that kind of battle. It would not win us the war but could lose the war to Japan.

In command of this theater less than ten days, he had been compelled to make several awesome decisions. He had listened to counsel, weighed Intelligence reports, gauged his ships and his men, and made the best decisions of which he was capable. They would soon prove wrong or right. An aircraft-carrier man, he had believed from the first that this would be a carrier showdown and had planned it accordingly.

As the *Enterprise* and *Hornet* forces steamed west, the main Japanese squadron veered toward them off the bottom tip of Guadalcanal. With the combatants two hundred fifty miles apart, the contest of carriers began. Distance left the mighty fire power of battleships and cruisers purely defensive against planes. Both sides launched air strikes almost simultaneously.

Against aerial attack, American commanders bunched their ships in order to throw up a common defensive curtain of lead. The Japanese held their vessels wide apart, believing this made them harder to hit. Their technique was effective until a ship was crippled and lost maneuverability; then, lacking protection from sister ships, she became an easier mark for the kill. The Americans' technique was born of necessity. Enemy planes came like showers of arrows, their fanatical pilots contemptuous of AA and racing straight into it. This fearlessness sprang from the Japanese belief that it was glorious to die for the Emperor, whereas Americans considered a dead hero of less value to his country than a live one.

The Battle of Santa Cruz was a contest between aircraft carriers lying two hundred fifty miles apart. Searching for the enemy, two *Big E* planes at 0830 on the twenty-sixth found the carrier *Shokaku* and the light carrier *Zuiho.* Empty flight decks indicated that their planes were off searching for the American ships. The fighters dived at *Zuiho,* placing two bombs that split open her stern. Thick smoke poured out.

At 1030 *Hornet* bombers put several one-thousand-pounders into the *Shokaku* and left her afire. Ten minutes later seventy-four *Enterprise* and *Hornet* fighters, dive bombers, and torpedo planes hurrying at the Japanese carriers ran into a wall of defending Zeroes. Eight dive bombers and two torpedo planes were shot down, but the others swept on. Grumman Avengers, peeling off at eight thousand feet, came out of the sun at the carrier *Zuikaku,* but damage, if any, was not great.

Meanwhile at 1010 the *Hornet* had received a violent fighter plane and dive bomber attack. Two huge bombs blasted open her flight deck, then four more exploded aboard her. Two torpedoes drilled into her waterline. A suicide plane smashed into her port bow. Five minutes more saw the *Hornet* afire on three decks, power and communications gone, dead in the water.

As the clock reached 1101 a *Hornet* flier spied a torpedo in the water headed for the destroyer *Porter.* Radio circuits were choked with traffic and he could not get her attention. Trying to warn the *Porter,* he flew down at her and promptly was taken under AA fire. At last his waggling wings somehow conveyed his warning—but too late. The torpedo's explosion opened a barn-door-size hole in the *Porter*'s thin skin and the sea poured in. Her crew began jumping overboard.

Nearby, the *Enterprise* was taking the heaviest pounding of her career, at one time being the target of twenty-four dive bombers. With her hundred four AA guns perched all over her spitting at them, two enemy planes blew apart and four turned away. But an enemy bomb lifted part of the *Big E*'s forward elevator platform high in the sky and jammed the mechanism. A near-miss ruptured a bilge fuel tank from which draining oil formed a second wake. A lookout spied three torpedoes abreast racing toward her. The *Big E* at full power kicked her stern to starboard and evaded the nearest torpedo by ten feet.

She was afire in a dozen places and holed in several, but her six hundred sixty-two watertight compartments provided a safety margin that kept her in action and steaming. Radar smashed, all communications gone, beginning to list, the *Big E* continued to take aboard orphan planes from the *Hornet* and fought on.

After a lull more attacks came at 1305. The battleship *South Dakota*'s accurate AA gunners shot down twenty-four bombers and torpedo planes – but one got through. Its five-hundred-pound bomb wrecked her forward turret and killed the gun crews. Flying bits of steel killed two men on her bridge and made a razorlike cut across the throat of Captain Gatch, her skipper. A quick-witted medical corpsman knelt and pinched the severed ends of his jugular vein while a doctor hastily sewed the artery together. Captain Gatch survived.

Mitsubishi and Aichi 99 planes continued their torpedo and bomb assaults. Our cruiser *San Juan* was partially disabled but remained in the fight. The *Hornet*, it appeared, might be saved. Three destroyers shouldered against her and began throwing a Niagara of water over her blazing flight deck while crewmen went below to fight smaller fires. But their effort was like waving nectar at bees. A Japanese torpedo plane found its target on her starboard side. The sea spurted between dozens of twisted plates and her list slowly bent to twenty degrees. The order rang through her gangways: "Abandon ship! Abandon ship!"

Each side had had enough. The action broke off.

We had lost one carrier, one destroyer, two hundred eighty-three men killed or missing, and seventy-four planes. Some of our plane losses were from launching or landing accidents, unavoidable in the heat of battle. The enemy lost two carriers, though both still floated, one damaged cruiser and a hundred planes in combat, plus an unknown number in operational accidents.

In relative strength our loss was considerably the greater. " If you call that victory," worried officers agreed, " one or two more like it are going to finish us." Washington shared their apprehension and saw to it that the news was withheld from the public until more decisive engagements were fought.

Halsey, however, remained supremely confident. He insisted that enemy losses were of greater significance than ours. Four of their air groups of highly trained pilots had been almost wiped out – men, he declared, whom Japan could not replace. And the two carriers knocked out had weakened Japanese air support for the coming Battle of Guadalcanal. His assurance buoyed up wavering members of his staff.

Our damaged ships lumbered southward for Nouméa, where all service branches were hastily assembling every available mechanic. The moment a new arrival's anchor splashed into the bay, repair gangs came swarming over her sides. Riveters, welders, carpenters, ship-fitters, and ordnance experts continued their labors around the clock because soon there was going to be more battle.

Now Halsey on a quick flight made his long-wanted visit to Guadalcanal. His aides welcomed this chance to let its defenders see him in person. Nothing was wrong with GI and dogface morale but sight of Old COMSOPAC himself would be sure to cause excitement and lend a new sense of strength. But Halsey, in one of his moods of excessive modesty, refused to be " on display," and wearing a spotted jungle coverall, stalked around Henderson Field looking like everyone else, and few Pfc's recognized him. Most of his time was spent conferring with General Vandegrift. During the Japanese bombing that night he was heard to scold himself, "You blamed coward!" and when this became known after his departure at least he caused a few thousand laughs.

Back on Nouméa he studied the estimate prepared by Intelligence. The struggle was still for Guadalcanal. Two days from now, November 11, the enemy were expected to begin their all-out assault. First would come a heavy aerial bombing. The night of the twelfth, heavy ships' twelve- and fourteen-inch guns would pitch high-explosive shells at Henderson Field. On the thirteenth, after an all-day air attack, troops would land. The Japanese armor would be two carriers, four battleships, five cruisers, thirty destroyers. They would shepherd twenty loaded troop transports and cargo ships.

Halsey's strength was scattered. Some he had committed to support Vandegrift and some, including the *Enterprise,* were still under repair. He had few warships remaining with which to contest the enemy thrust. What little he had, he meant to use fully.

At 0530 the morning of the eleventh, Admiral Scott brought three cargo vessels to anchor off Lunga Point on Guadalcanal, guarded by one light cruiser and four destroyers. They had four hours of unloading before they were attacked by dive bombers. All the Japanese were shot down, but the transports were damaged, one seriously; she wavered off for Espiritu under escort of a destroyer. The other two continued their unloading all night.

On the twelfth Admiral Turner brought four transports guarded by two cruisers and four destroyers. Unloading was interrupted two hours by torpedo planes but was 90 percent finished when Turner had to pull away because a strong enemy force was approaching down the channel.

Scott now added his meager strength to Admiral Callaghan's, his senior. Callaghan had brought in two heavy cruisers and one light one, and six destroyers. But the forces that went out were only five cruisers and eight destroyers. They were outnumbered and outgunned, but the hope was that Callaghan could stand off the Japanese until the *Enterprise* arrived with air support the next morning, the thirteenth.

With Halsey's policy of ATTACK REPEAT ATTACK in mind, Callaghan on his flagship, the cruiser *San Francisco,* went searching the Slot northwest. As he moved into Lengo Channel at 0124 hours that dark morning of the thirteenth, *Helena*'s radar picked up three groups of ships about fifteen miles away.

Was this accurate? Land masses nearby confused radar readings. There was no moon, no stars. TBS was unintelligible. The task force crept on. Suddenly, through the dark, searchlights pinned the whole line of ships. They found themselves between two groups of the enemy at the point-blank range for big guns of three thousand yards.

" Shoot out those lights! " shouted Captain Jenkins on the cruiser *Atlanta.*

A shell smashed her bridge, wounding him. It killed Admiral Scott and sixteen other men. Out of control, the *Atlanta* zigzagged into disastrous bow-to-stern raking by the five-inch guns of two Japanese destroyers.

Far south at Nouméa aboard the *Argonne,* once again Bill Halsey strode the deck, snatched at every radio message, gulped down hot coffee, rushed to the chart room for still more scrutiny of the battle area. He had ordered Callaghan and Scott with their inadequate armor into Lengo Channel. Had he blundered?

Although the engagement lasted only twenty-four minutes, Admiral King later pronounced it " one of the most furious sea battles ever fought." To Halsey, and to the men fighting enemy on two sides, it seemed to last hours. Why was there no word from Callaghan? Was *San Francisco* still afloat?

A dispatch from the *Portland:*

STEERING ROOM FLOODED AND RUDDER JAMMED HARD RIGHT BY TORPEDO HIT STARBOARD QUARTER X CANNOT STEER WITH ENGINES X REQUEST TOW

Tow? Where could Halsey find any kind of vessel capable of going up there to tow *Portland*?

From the *Atlanta:*

HELP NEEDED

From the *Helena:*

HELENA, SAN FRANCISCO, JUNEAU (CRUISERS), O BANNON, FLETCHER, STERETT (DESTROYERS) PROCEEDING COURSE ONE SEVEN FIVE (RETIRING TOWARD ESPIRITU) X HELENA SENIOR SHIP X ALL SHIPS DAMAGED X REQUEST MAXIMUM AIR COVER

Still no word from Admiral Callaghan. If the *Helena* had become the senior ship, then Callaghan must be dead. He was dead, killed by a smashing salvo from the battleship *Hiyei.*

The hours dragged past. What damage had been done to the enemy? The thin trickle of information seemed increasingly ominous.

Late that afternoon a roundup message came from Guadalcanal:

TEN MILES NORTH SAVO FIVE ENEMY DESTROYERS ATTEMPTING ASSIST KONGO-CLASS BATTLESHIP WHICH HAS BEEN HIT BY SEVEN TORPEDOES AND 1000 LB BOMB X AFTER PART OF SHIP BURNING X SHIP BELIEVED HOSTILE DESTROYER BEACHED NORTH COAST OLEVUGA ISLAND X LARGE VESSEL BURNING INDISPENSABLE STRAIT X USS CUSHING BURNING FIVE MILES SE SAVO AND USS MONSSEN DEAD IN WATER BOTH ABANDONED X ATLANTA AND PORTLAND BADLY DAMAGED X USS LAFFEY SUNK X 700 SURVIVORS PICKED UP X 25% OF THESE WOUNDED

Our cost, when at last Halsey could count it, was one cruiser and five destroyers, with all other vessels involved damaged. The enemy lost the battleship *Hiyei* and two destroyers and had five other ships damaged.

Yet the job assigned had been done. The Japanese schedule had been upset. Said CINCPAC's official report:

This action . . . was a turning point in the Solomon Islands campaign. Had the powerful enemy fleet succeeded in its mis-

> sion of bombarding our airfield on Guadalcanal, the task of preventing a major enemy attack and landing of large-scale reinforcements would have been much more difficult, if not impossible. . . . The resolution with which Rear Admirals Callaghan and Scott led the ships in, the well-directed fire and courage of our personnel, merit the highest praise.

If the Lengo Channel action was a turning point, Bill Halsey did not know it then. To him it appeared only another round in the enemy's insistence on seizing Guadalcanal.

[Chapter 12]

# Four Stars

WHAT REMAINED of Admiral Callaghan's force obviously was in no condition for another fight. Yet the enemy must not be permitted to bring down their main invasion armada and make good their bombardment, followed by plane-protected troop landings. The Marines' heroic defense of Guadalcanal then would end in disaster, and Japan would have the grip she sought on the entire Southwest Pacific.

The *Enterprise*'s forward deck elevator remained jammed from bombing but her two after elevators functioned. She had other damage and while she rushed up from Nouméa three repair gangs continued feverishly at work on her. Midday of the thirteenth she began to reach out air attacks on the stricken but still floating battleship *Hiyei.*

Halsey ordered Admiral Kinkaid, the *Big E*'s commander, to detach two battleships and four destroyers under Admiral Lee. Replacing Callaghan's force, Lee would speed to Savo Island and prepare to intercept the main enemy invasion fleet. Because Savo waters were treacherous with shoals and crosscurrents, Halsey was aware that the Naval War College would not approve this risk of capital ships; nevertheless, here was a gamble he felt compelled to take. He comforted himself by recalling Lord Nelson's famous note to his commanders before the Battle of Trafalgar: "No Captain can do very wrong if he places his Ship alongside that of the Enemy."

Kinkaid acknowledged his order with:

FROM LEE'S PRESENT POSITION IMPOSSIBLE TO REACH SAVO BEFORE 0800 TOMORROW

Reading this on the deck of the *Argonne*, Halsey groaned. Eight tomorrow morning would be too late to block enemy progress to bombardment position. Sure enough, dawn next day, the fourteenth, brought him a dispatch from General Vandegrift:

HENDERSON BEING HEAVILY SHELLED

But after eighty minutes, strangely, the shelling ceased. The enemy ships got under way. Not until afterward did Halsey learn that a squadron of PT (patrol torpedo) boats under Lieutenant Robinson, dashing over from Tulagi, had in bright morning sunshine actually chased away six Japanese cruisers and five destroyers.

The shelling cost Henderson Field three planes wrecked and seventeen damaged. Working at top speed, Marines in a few hours filled the runway bomb craters while air and ground crews were repairing, fueling, and arming every usable plane. Including three stray *Enterprise* fighters, twenty surged after the withdrawing Japanese. They overtook them and scored hits on two cruisers. *Enterprise* air patrols noticed this celebration, flew over for a look, and whistled up sixteen torpedo planes to assist.

Assuming the principal invasion force to be on its way south down the Slot, Halsey that morning had ordered the *Enterprise* group northward on course to intercept. Admiral Lee waited in the vicinity of Savo. Joining, they soon confronted two enemy groups. The leading one had three heavy cruisers, one light, an aircraft carrier, and a destroyer. The second was thirteen destroyers protecting eleven troop-laden transports.

Eleven troop transports! On his headquarters plotting board scores of miles to the south, Bill Halsey spied opportunity with a large O. Though his was the underdog force, here was a rare chance for a kill. He kept the air sizzling with instructions to seize it.

In typical Halsey strategy he had the *Big E*'s and Admiral Lee's forces fall into two parallel files: the *Enterprise* group a hundred miles out, Lee's moderately inshore. Thus *Big E* planes could reach over the protecting wall of Lee's battleships to make their strikes. Halsey's final dispatch read:

YOUR OBJECTIVE TRANSPORTS

Everything within reach that could fly was thrown into this chance to smash the enemy. The *Enterprise* lofted every fighter, dive bomber, and torpedo plane except for her irreducible defense group. Marine fighters sped up from Henderson Field. Army B-17's came roaring over from Espiritu. Starting at 1000 hours, " Buzzard Patrol " went after Japanese.

The enemy carrier's air umbrella was not enough to weather this storm. The AA fire of Japanese warships, although heavy as always, could not stave off the fierce assaults on both themselves and their transports. One Marine fighter pilot diving at a troop ship saw her deck seething with soldiers who had no place to hide. Kicking his Wildcat's rudder to the right, then to the left, he sprayed his wing machine guns at them like two garden hoses. Then he placed a pair of two-hundred-fifty-pound bombs amidships.

After the fighters came the wave of dive bombers. Meanwhile, torpedo planes drilled their deadly tin fish into the troop transports' high sides.

As the first big liner took a sharp list, men poured off her like ants off a board. Those who drowned quickly were fortunate. Burst fuel tanks poured oil over the sea, and flames raced across it to engulf all floating rafts and wreckage.

It was not a pleasant sight to the attackers. But it was war. Time and again our planes returned to base or carrier, refueled, rearmed, and sped away back to the carnage. " It's like shooting fish in a barrel," grimly reported one pilot.

As the afternoon waned, two burning Japanese transports became glowing, cherry-red steel hulks. Four others and one heavy cruiser were sunk. Another four transports and two destroyers, all crippled, crawled away. Two Marine pilots spied a speedboat hurrying from one sinking ship, guessed it contained high officers, and with their machine guns chewed it to bits.

At twilight the Buzzard Patrol fliers, exhausted and almost sick with what they had had to do, called it a day.

Next morning a scout plane discovered the four damaged transports beached off Tassafaronga, feverishly unloading men and supplies. Fighter planes and bombers called to the scene gave almost a repeat of yesterday's performance as they strafed the troops and blew up their fuel and ammunition dumps. The planes retired to let our destroyer *Meade* slide cautiously to what Halsey called "popgun range" for her five-inch guns to complete the wrecking. The few Japanese who succeeded in struggling ashore fled into the jungle. Lacking food or water, they must have perished there.

Almost as if the enemy failed to realize the enormity of their losses, they sent in yet another force. It was sighted the afternoon of the fourteenth a hundred fifty miles away, giving Lee ample time to resume his position near Savo. The word reached Henderson Field of another sea battle impending, and GI's and dogfaces left their foxholes to rush for choice seats on the high bluff overlooking Lunga Point.

A few miles out there in the darkness, the watchers knew, Lee's task force cruised, waiting. At midnight soaring flares that splashed the sky located each battle group to the other.

The pattern of the fight was like that in which Admirals Callaghan and Scott had been killed, except that this time it was Japanese who were caught in the vise. They had nine destroyers, the battleship *Kirishima,* and four cruisers.

As the battlewagon *Kirishima* swung into view through the north passage, the *South Dakota* and *Washington*'s sixteen-inch rifles pounded into action. Watchers ashore stopped their ears while they counted the rosettes of fire slashing out in volley. Several shells set the Japanese battleship burning and smoke enveloped her. When the breeze nudged a hole in her shroud *Kirishima* had sunk. Her cruisers and destroyers charged at their tormentors for revenge.

"The water was alive with their tin fish," said the skipper of the U.S.S. *Gwin*. The Japanese sank three of our destroyers. But they could not withstand the tremendous fire power of our two battleships, and breaking formation, they fled. The action gave birth to a name for the waters southeast of Savo, "Iron Bottom Bay."

Two weeks later the Japanese attempted to sneak another troop landing at Tassafaronga, but Halsey, with forces strengthened by then, turned them back. For all practical purposes, those Marines perched on the bluff had witnessed the last act of the Battle of Guadalcanal. It was not until February 5, however, that Army General Patch, who replaced Vandegrift on the island, rang down the curtain with the crisp announcement:

ORGANIZED RESISTANCE ON GUADALCANAL HAS CEASED

In the great contest of strength the enemy had sixteen ships sunk and at least nine others made ready for months of work in drydock. The United States had ten ships sunk and seven damaged.

In naval personnel we lost fewer than one hundred, the enemy twice as many. Japanese troop losses were between fifteen and twenty thousand, ours at Henderson Field twelve hundred killed, twenty-six hundred wounded. Almost every man who served there developed malaria. But Guadalcanal was ours.

The Battle of Midway, which stopped the Japanese advance eastward in the Central Pacific, had been the first turning point in the war. The second was the Battle of Coral Sea, which blunted Japanese progress in the Southwest Pacific. Now in the South Pacific further expansion was denied to the Rising Sun

Empire dream of a Greater East Asia Co-Prosperity Sphere.

Halsey recommended decorations for a large number of participants in the struggle for Guadalcanal. One that gave him special pleasure was the Presidential Unit Citation for his old flagship, *Enterprise*. Reported many times on enemy radio to have been sunk, she was as ready as ever for battle after taking part in eight major actions in less than a year.

The messages from President Roosevelt, Secretary of the Navy Knox, and Admiral King led the shower of congratulations from the States. Elizabeth, New Jersey, where Halsey was born, held "Halsey Day"; public buildings were decorated, schools closed early, and church bells were rung. Echoing all the thanks, he broadcast this message throughout his theater of war:

From: Halsey
To: All ships SOPAC, all com'dg generals SOPAC

TO THE SUPERB OFFICERS AND MEN UNDER THE SEA AND ON THE SEA AND IN THE AIR WHO HAVE IN THE PAST FEW DAYS PERFORMED SUCH MAGNIFICENT FEATS FOR THE US: YOUR NAMES HAVE BEEN WRITTEN IN GOLDEN LETTERS IN THE PAGES OF HISTORY AND YOU HAVE WON THE EVERLASTING GRATITUDE OF YOUR COUNTRYMEN X NO HONOR FOR YOU COULD BE TOO GREAT X MY PRIDE IN YOU IS BEYOND EXPRESSION X MAGNIFICENTLY DONE X TO THE GLORIOUS DEAD: HAIL HEROES, REST WITH GOD X BLESS YOU ALL.

Three days after the battle, Halsey's aides scouring Nouméa finally obtained four two-star silver insignia donated by a major general of the Marines, which they welded into two circles of four stars each. These would have to suffice until regulation Navy pins could be had. The service never at one time had counted more than a quartet of four-star admirals, but President Roosevelt nominated Bill Halsey to be our fifth and Congress immediately approved.

[Chapter 13]

# Breathing Spell

THE ENEMY WITHDRAWAL brought a lull welcomed by the entire South Pacific command. At last the First Marines, elements of the Second, and the Americal Division on Guadalcanal could be relieved by Army's Twenty-fifth Infantry and ferried to Australia for a long-overdue rest. In early 1943 new troop units arrived from the States. The Navy added supply and combat vessels as mainland shipyards, running in high gear, began to produce enough so that some strength could be diverted from our war in Europe to our war in the Pacific.

Halsey found time to survey and organize the command he had taken over from Admiral Ghormley. One of his first orders was to dispense with wearing neckties. "We're not on parade and they're uncomfortable in this climate," he told his chief of staff, Miles Browning. "Anyway, the Army doesn't wear them, and I want all the men to feel they're on the same team."

To impress this point he personally warned his subordinate commanders: "I'll tolerate no friction between services. We're here to fight Japs, not each other. If there is any sign of interservice lack of cooperation, we'll dye all uniforms a neutral gray and print on the seat of the pants in capital letters, 'SOUTH PACIFIC FIGHTING FORCE.'"

His next step was to find more space for his headquarters. The repair ship *Argonne* was too small and too crowded. He sent Julian Brown in full-dress uniform to make a formal request for space ashore to M. Montchamps, Free French Governor of New Caledonia. As Brown explained his errand Montchamps listened without enthusiasm. " What," he inquired, " will you give us in return? "

Brown's eyes flashed. " Protection," he snapped, " as we Americans have protected you from the Japanese to this moment! "

The Governor said he would consider the matter, but despite reminders, kept avoiding any decision. Losing patience, Halsey ordered his entire headquarters staff to move. Without bothering to inform Montchamps they occupied the former offices of the High Commissioner of Free France, a gentleman so disliked that the New Caledonians had locked him up. For their living quarters, Halsey and his officers took over the home of the former Japanese consul, who was being held in Australia. Situated on a breeze-swept hilltop, it contained the inevitable painting of Fujiyama and dwarf pine trees in pots. Its furniture, linens, and dishware were luxurious. When a mess attendant broke a soup tureen, instead of bringing scowls, the accident was waved away.

" Forget it. That stuff belongs to the Nip."

In this more efficient setup Halsey could take advantage of an occasional hour for relaxation. An early riser, frequently he went for a swim before breakfast, then entered his office at seven thirty. Unless interrupted, he labored there until five when he might have another swim or a social hour. Often after dinner he returned to his desk.

Wherever he was, it was his policy to get some daily exercise. On shipboard this might be calisthenics or handball on the flight deck. On Nouméa he often jogtrotted a mile along the beach, rested, then trotted back. Swimming was his preference, and he called it the ideal exercise.

Paper work was Halsey's particular dislike, and whatever he disliked he tackled first, to get it over with. He expected subordinates to do the same, and needless delay could bring that steady, searching look. " I can forgive occasional stupidity," he growled, " but there's never any excuse for put-offingness."

He was, on the whole, even-tempered, especially considering the responsibilities that burdened his shoulders. A believer in delegating authority, he enlarged his staff until the Operations section alone numbered twenty-five officers. But final decisions affecting the safety of the United States, the lives of soldiers, sailors, and Marines, and hundreds of millions of dollars worth of equipment could only be made by COMSOPAC himself.

Forever uppermost was the problem of strategy toward the enemy. How were their forces distributed now? What immediate action did they plan, toward what long-range goal? Map-room conferences with advisers from each service were held daily. Intelligence information was weighed, armor and logistics discussed. Hating any defensive position, Bill Halsey constantly pressured his officers with: " Where can we hit them? How soon? "

Battle plans to meet every imaginable situation were drawn up in detail down to the last fighter plane, the last five-hundred-pound bomb, and the probable weather. These bulky documents were filed, and according to equipment on hand, continuously brought up to date. When need arose, a battle plan could be spread on a table and the wheels of each service set spinning to fulfill its every requirement.

Important information about the enemy held top priority on Halsey's attention at all hours, whether he was at his desk or asleep. He was in constant communication with Admiral Nimitz at Pearl Harbor and with SOWESPAC concerning strategy, ships, men, and supplies. A commander's never-ending worry was to have the right kind of forces at the right place at the right time. Lack of enough Higgins boats or heavy naval guns or torpedo planes could lose a battle, even a war.

In the last analysis all of Bill Halsey's concerns had to do with human nature, with men. His topmost task was to outthink and outfight the men of Japan. But in his own forces there were instances of incompetence that had to be remedied. Now and then a dispute over authority worked its way up the chain of command for the Admiral's decision. As in any large organization there were a few troublemakers, "goldbrick artists," thieves, and cheats. Courts-martial decided their cases, but any verdict concerning a more serious offense such as dereliction of duty came to Halsey to review. When he had to approve some young American's sentence to a long term in military prison, he was known to sit staring down at his desk, his eyes glistening with tears.

During the bitter Solomons campaign ugly rumors circulating in the United States made Bill Halsey's lonely responsibility the harder to bear. He was incompetent, so the gossip went. He was a butcher who needlessly sent men to their death against hopeless odds. Why hadn't he delivered reinforcements to those Marines at Henderson Field? What was Halsey doing, holding the Navy back, out of danger, while he left those poor dogfaces to be murdered? Or take the cruiser *Juneau*'s sinking off Savo Island. Why didn't that nearby cruiser turn back for rescue? More than a hundred *Juneau* men were left struggling in the water.

"That skipper did what Halsey told him to. What does he care about a hundred men?" ran the criticism. Not told in the press was that immediately after the action Halsey relieved the cruiser captain; but later, after a full investigation, he returned the man to duty.

"Taking him off his bridge was wrong. It was an emotional decision," Halsey confessed. "Remember, it was dark that night. Our side was taking an awful lambasting. The man did his duty, a heartbreaking one. He knew that if he stayed for rescue, he would probably lose his own ship. Then our loss would not have been a hundred lives but several hundred."

The men of COMSOPAC were making no complaint. Nor were top commanders at Pearl Harbor and in Washington. They understood that we had to stand up and be slugged in order to buy delay until we could become strong enough to win. But on the mainland five thousand miles away half information and rumor too often were accepted as fact. Much of it originated with Tokyo Rose, an around-the-clock radio program beamed at America. Its innuendoes were sly and mean, offered as "news" or "the truth." Too many Americans swallowed this propaganda and bristled with resentment. In time, word of their feelings got back to Halsey.

Because of the need for secrecy in all his operations, he could not defend himself. His only consolation was to be told of some officer or enlisted man who was heard to boast: "What outfit am I in? Listen, I'm with Bill Halsey." But the knowledge that some of the very people at home whom he was protecting called him "butcher" robbed the admiral of sleep. For a memorable two days it actually made him ill.

Always blunt and explosive in his opinions, he aroused criticism in the United States with a New Year's Day interview granted correspondents on Nouméa. We now had the initiative wrested away from Japan, he declared. The Rising Sun would find itself set by the end of 1943. He added scorching personal comments on Emperor Hirohito, Prime Minister Tojo, the Japanese Navy, and Nipponese everywhere. Although his staff censor softened his language, it still impressed Washington as too strong. Several newspaper editorials called his prophecy that the war would conclude in a year "unjustified and downright reckless."

Halsey's real opinion was that the war could not end in one year, perhaps not in three. Nevertheless, a few days later on a visit to New Zealand he made a similar statement. Prime Minister Fraser had confided that his countrymen still feared a Japanese breakthrough and kept demanding their divisions returned from North Africa. But Mr. Churchill and President Roosevelt insisted that the troops could not be spared from General Montgomery's forces shakily holding German and Italian armies at bay. Besides, there were no transports to return them.

"I don't want to jeopardize the Allied cause," Mr. Fraser assured Halsey. "But my war cabinet may force me to ask for our troops back. Would you care to repeat your New Year's opinion? It might help people to see matters differently. I have a number of editors and reporters waiting at your hotel."

The resulting interview printed in the *New Zealand Herald* said in part:

> Admiral Halsey stood confidently to his recently cabled prediction of a complete Allied victory in 1943. . . . "We have 363 days to fulfill my prediction and we are going to do it."
> Questioned whether he was satisfied with the progress of operations against the Japanese, he replied, "We have their measure in the air, on and under the water, and on land. . . . They are not supermen, though they try to make us believe they are."
> "What do you expect Japan's next move will be?" Admiral Halsey was asked.
> "Japan's next move will be to retreat," he said. "A start has been made to make them retreat. They will not be able to stop going back."
> His confidence was clearly immense. . . . It became very clear why it is said of Admiral "Pudge" Halsey by his officers and men that they would follow him to Hell. He is a man whose confidence could clearly win battles.

In making his assertions, some of which he knew were exaggerations, Halsey was not seeking to impress the people of the United States. His words were intended for Allied ears in the South Pacific. He realized that his sailors, fliers, Marines, and Army men were battleworn, their morale wavering. They longed to be quit of jungle heat and insects and the blank dreariness of tiny islands – wondered if they were forgotten by the people at home.

As for Australians and New Zealanders, Halsey knew that they had cause for their anxiety. It arose from the myth of Japanese invincibility, and this had to be exploded. The Pearl Harbor sneak raid, the capture of the Philippines, and the Japanese rapid expansion over most of the Far East had made people fear the enemy had overwhelming strength, that they were supermen.

"They aren't," Halsey snapped. "They're only tricky little devils, and from now on you'll see them running."

His very boldness cheered up our forces and South Pacific civilians. Evidently what he said also gave the Japanese pause, for they did not attack for six months and trebled their Intelligence efforts to find out what gave Halsey such confidence. Meanwhile, Tokyo Rose broadcast the list of tortures awaiting the capture of Halsey. When he got back to Nouméa, two of his officers acted out a pantomime, and when he asked what it meant, they grinned.

"We're stirring up a Tokyo Rose cauldron for you, Admiral. Boiling oil!"

When COMSOPAC learned that a high Japanese officer would be landed at Cape Esperance by submarine on a certain night, our Navy commander in the area was notified with the suggestion: "Get him."

In a few hours a dispatch arrived: "Sank sub x Important gent still aboard."

A surprise night torpedo plane raid in the Slot sank our heavy cruiser *Chicago* and damaged the destroyer *Lavallette.* This was the heaviest action during January, 1943. By the end of the month, port and ground training facilities and several small airfields had been developed on Efate, Espiritu Santo, and close to Guadalcanal in the Tulagi-Purvis Bay area. New ships and planes replaced well-worn older ones. Undoubtedly the enemy too were rushing completion of new aircraft carriers and warships and adding muscle to their island bases; but offsetting their buildup, for the first time Halsey had at his disposal six powerful task forces.

The day was nearing to begin an offensive.

## [Chapter 14]

# Advance on Rabaul

INFORMATION about enemy planes and movements came to Allied commands from many sources. No doubt the United States had spies in Japan but because of the striking difference in appearance between Orientals and Caucasians, these must have been relatively few. Skippers of submarines hunting in enemy waters, pilots of aircraft, and the masters of Navy surface vessels all reported their observations, which were correlated by Intelligence. But for on-the-spot information concerning enemy activities on the many South Pacific islands, no source was more valuable to our strategists than the " coast watchers."

Coast watchers were all Australians or New Zealanders. They probably did not total two hundred men. Before the war they had been managers of South Pacific coconut plantations or masters of interisland trading schooners, and when the tide of Japanese forces washed southward, they hid in the jungles. There each man worked alone, risking his life to serve the Allies without expectation of pay or recognition.

They knew their areas and the waters around them well. Often for months without relief, a coast watcher kept vigil several hundred miles inside enemy lines. His equipment was a few supplies, a weapon or two, and a portable radio transmitter. Using a code name, he broadcast his daily or weekly report at an agreed hour, then hastily moved so as to elude Japanese radio locators.

Aided by friendly natives, coast watchers rescued many of our downed fliers. They reported them, cared for them, and kept them hidden until some means of rescue could be devised. One who kept a record saved over thirty airmen from capture.

The enemy maintained constant searches for the coast watchers. They tortured natives to make them tell their whereabouts and if a watcher was captured, the Japanese, as a warning, forced natives to witness his agonized death. In spite of all this, there were few betrayals. Ill treatment by the invaders made the Japanese generally hated, whereas the coast watchers were the native islanders' proved friends and could usually count on the natives' loyalty.

On Bougainville, in an effort to stamp out these volunteer observers, the enemy assembled forty-five trained dogs to hunt them down. A watcher on the island radioed the location of the kennels, and one night from the nearest American base a fighter plane responded. A direct hit with a two-hundred-fifty-pound bomb brought word on the next broadcast,

"Thanks. No more dogs."

Many local tongues were spoken among the island people, but most who had worked on plantations knew a common one, pidgin English. Every American flier carried a paper on which were a dozen phrases in pidgin which would be useful if he was downed and encountered natives:

> If the Japanese come, hide the white man and give them false information.
> *Sapos Japan ikam kilostu yupaka haitim masta nau giamonim ol Japan.*
>
> Later you will be paid for all these services.
> *Biaen igat pe ikemap long ol dispala samting.*

The securing of Guadalcanal marked the end of the struggle for the southern islands in the Solomon chain. Bill Halsey was impatient to begin his offensive to win the northern half dominated by Rabaul, the most powerful Japanese stronghold in hundreds of miles.

His first step in ELKTON, as the campaign was coded, to begin May 15, called for seizure of Munda on the large island of New Georgia. Munda subdued, the next move would be against Bougainville. Once Bougainville was overcome, an assault could be mounted against Rabaul farther north.

The enemy had fifty thousand troops on Rabaul by February, 1943, together with transports to move them, cargo ships to supply them, and warships to guard them. With these they expected to win back Guadalcanal. But over on the north coast of New Guinea, General MacArthur's Australian-American troops had unexpectedly given the enemy a mauling that made their High Command reconsider. Ought they to divert their expeditionary force to New Guinea? Or was it more important to keep them, as planned, in the Solomons?

They decided to send their invasion strength to New Guinea. The force lasted there just a month, until the Battle of the Bismarck Sea. But Rabaul was considered still impregnable with its five well-stocked airfields, an ample segment of the fleet, and heavy guns strategically placed in the surrounding mountains.

The imaginary line dividing Halsey and MacArthur's commands ran northeast-southwest across the middle of the seven-hundred-mile-long Solomon chain. Halsey's responsibility was to CINCPAC at Pearl Harbor and COMINCH in Washington. MacArthur, being Army, was responsible to his headquarters in Washington. Control of all forces was vested there in the Joint Chiefs of Staff.

For a springboard to Operation ELKTON, Halsey needed to build an airfield on tiny Woodlark Island. It lay only three hundred miles from Rabaul, two hundred from Bougainville, and within bomber range of Munda. But Woodlark was in SOWES–PAC, so Halsey sent his request for permission up the Navy line of command. It was passed on to the Joint Chiefs, who

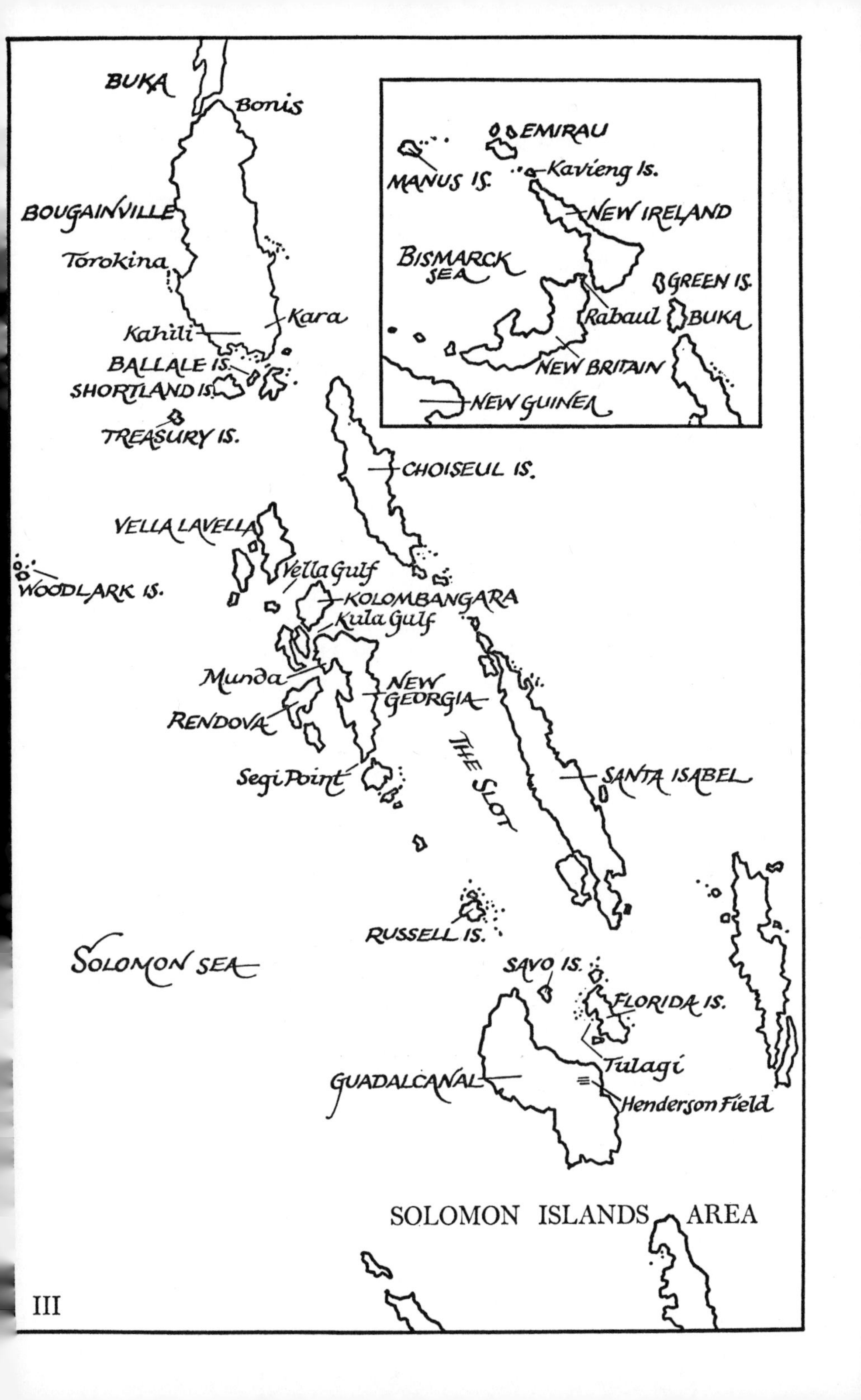
BUKA
Bonis
BOUGAINVILLE
Torokina
Kara
Kahili
BALLALE IS.
SHORTLAND IS.
TREASURY IS.
EMIRAU
MANUS IS.
Kavieng Is.
NEW IRELAND
BISMARCK SEA
GREEN IS.
Rabaul
BUKA
NEW BRITAIN
NEW GUINEA
CHOISEUL IS.
VELLA LAVELLA
WOODLARK IS.
Vella Gulf
KOLOMBANGARA
Kula Gulf
Munda
NEW GEORGIA
RENDOVA
THE SLOT
Segi Point
SANTA ISABEL
RUSSELL IS.
SOLOMON SEA
SAVO IS.
FLORIDA IS.
Tulagi
GUADALCANAL
Henderson Field
SOLOMON ISLANDS AREA
III

approved it subject to MacArthur's agreement, and Halsey flew to Brisbane, Australia, to discuss the matter.

A veteran of forty years of distinguished Army service, Douglas MacArthur was a tall, fit-looking, black-haired man of sixty-three who appeared ten years younger. His manner was grave, his general knowledge impressive, and his voice like that of a trained Shakespearean actor. The two leaders formed an instant liking for each other. Typically, while they talked, MacArthur paced his office clutching a corncob pipe, which he seldom smoked, pausing now and then to aim its stem at something on the wall map. Halsey listened from his chair until, growing excited, he jumped up and paced the floor in another direction. When they collided, each roused from his concentration, grinned, and turned to sit down.

After the conference they separated to consult with their staffs, then met again. MacArthur readily endorsed the Woodlark project. They went on to make general plans for the whole future struggle in the Pacific. It was MacArthur's obsession to recapture the Philippines and Halsey's to sink every ship in the Imperial Japanese Navy.

Back on Nouméa, Halsey found a surprise. Our code experts had learned that Admiral Isoroku Yamamoto, Commander in Chief of the Japanese Navy, was coming to visit the Solomons. He would reach Ballale, south of Bougainville, at 0945 on April 18. When that morning dawned, eighteen P-38's of Army's 339th Fighter Squadron raced from Henderson Field to welcome him.

Yamamoto's Betty plane neared Ballale on schedule. It was accompanied by another Betty and six Zekes (late model Zeroes). Lieutenant Colonel Thomas Lanphier, Jr., sent the Admiral's plane spinning down in flames, and the man who had planned the sneak attack on Pearl Harbor was out of the war he had started. The second Betty was also downed, and one of the Zekes.

Halsey had begun occasional ship bombardment of Munda in

January. As soon as Woodlark became an operational field Munda was bombed by air. Reacting, the Japanese one day threw more than sixty fighters and sixty bombers against Guadalcanal. A hundred Army, Navy, and Marine planes rose to challenge them. The result was a slaughter: the Japanese lost one hundred and seven planes, whereas the Americans lost only six.

"I've often said one American can lick seven Japs," Bill Halsey exulted. "I was wrong. One American pilot can knock eighteen Japs out of the sky!"

The Guadalcanal campaign had shown that the heroic island coast watchers lacked enough military background to recognize certain things the Allies needed to know. In preparation for ELKTON a combat reconnaissance school was organized with Marine and Army instructors. "Students" were stealthily airlifted by night or arrived in small boats. They were taught how to identify various kinds of ships and planes, types of heavy guns, and to estimate troop numbers. Returning to their islands, the information they supplied was used in ELKTON's every move.

Bombing was stepped up from Woodlark and another island. The first New Georgia landing on June 21 took the enemy by surprise at Segi Point forty miles from Munda, which the Fourth Marine Raiders occupied without firing a shot. Immediately the Seabees, the Navy's construction service, hurried ashore. In eleven days their bulldozers cleared several hundred acres of jungle and completed an airstrip of crushed coral. This was only one of the Seabees' island-hopping building jobs that made possible quick and priceless land-based aerial support. Later, when Halsey was asked what modern tools he believed helped most to win the war, he named: submarines, radar, airplanes, and bulldozers, in that order.

Rendova came next, seven miles off Munda. Thirty-two American fighter planes warded off enemy attacks while six transports unloaded and 105mm. howitzers quickly set up began replying to Munda artillery. As the transports steamed away, twenty-eight Japanese planes attacked and one put a torpedo into the *McCawley,* in peacetime a handsome passenger liner. All the enemy planes were shot down. The *McCawley* was under tow when three more torpedoes finished her. They came from a PT boat whose skipper had mistaken her silhouette.

ELKTON saw other blunders. Before the operation began, Halsey removed a Marine major general for incompetence. During it the 43d Infantry, advancing behind a barrage from four destroyers near shore, became stalled. Although the 43d was in its first battle, the trouble was chiefly with its leadership. When General Harmon replaced the commanding general, the men pushed forward again.

During the four landings from assault barges at various points on the island there were mixups of units, reinforcements, and command. True, the well-entrenched enemy fought with their usual ferocity. Nevertheless, in sulfurous language Halsey pointed out that fifteen thousand United States troops had been expected to defeat nine thousand Japanese, yet before New Georgia was secured he had to pour in nearly fifty thousand. He called the island "a graveyard of reputations."

In Kula Gulf at the north end of New Georgia, Admiral Ainsworth, with three light cruisers and four destroyers, intercepted a night run in the Slot of the Tokyo Express. We lost the *Helena* to torpedoes in a four-hour battle. A week later Ainsworth, with three cruisers and six additional destroyers, met the Express again in the same waters. Our loss was the destroyer *Gwin* and three cruisers badly damaged, the enemy's loss, one cruiser. The cost to us was high, though it stopped further use of Kula Gulf to supply Japanese garrisons.

From General Griswold on August 5 came the dispatch:

OUR GROUND FORCES HAVE WRESTED MUNDA FROM THE JAPS AND PRESENT IT TO YOU AS SOLE OWNER

On August 7, Halsey's son, also named William Frederick, an officer aboard the carrier *Saratoga,* hitched a plane ride to Nouméa for his first visit in more than a year with his father. But two days after young Bill enplaned to return to duty, Halsey senior sat reading a report when his chief of staff entered, looking worried.

He handed the Admiral a tragic bulletin. Bill junior's plane was down somewhere in the hundreds of square miles along the route back to the *Saratoga.*

Halsey's cheeks paled, but his expression did not change. " I suppose the routine search is being made? "

" Yes, sir." The officer hesitated. " Admiral, do you desire that additional effort be made in this case? "

" Certainly not. My son is a sailor like anybody else. We do our best for every man within the limits of security." He went back to reading the report. " If anything turns up, let me know."

Several days later a search plane did find young Halsey and his companions floating on a rubber raft. The day was Friday the thirteenth.

" I've always been leery of that day," Halsey admitted, " since a turret explosion aboard the old *Missouri.* At last I know it's turned lucky for me."

About this time Halsey learned that Mrs. Eleanor Roosevelt, wife of the President, was due to arrive on her tour of the South and Southwest war theaters. Annoyed, he grumbled that he could not spare " fighting men to keep the Japs from grabbing her." He resented having to put on a necktie and when he met her plane, he smiled but made it known that he could fight a war better without having to entertain ladies.

Mrs. Roosevelt wore the uniform of the Red Cross, for which she had long been an ardent worker. Asking nothing except shelter, she set about walking miles to visit the sick and wounded. In one twelve-hour day she went through every ward of two Navy hospitals, ferried by small boat to an island officers' rest home, returned and inspected an Army hospital, reviewed the Second Marine Raiders of which her son James had been executive officer, wrote down dozens of messages to be relayed to families at home, spoke at a service club, shook hands with two hundred men at a reception, and was guest of honor at a dinner.

The Shore Police guarding her declared themselves exhausted. " The dame is running us ragged! "

Not only did she visit hospitals, Halsey learned when he accompanied her to one, but seeming unhurried, Mrs. Roosevelt paused to visit every patient, including some whose wounds made them gruesome to look at. She asked their names, about wives or sweethearts, and how soon they expected to get well. By request she pinned medals on a number of wounded to whom they had been awarded. Escorting her to her plane, Halsey apologized for his cool reception. He told her, " Mrs. Roosevelt, you have pumped up morale here at least ten degrees."

Kolombangara Island, north of New Georgia, was the next stepping-stone toward Rabaul. The outlook for its capture was dismaying, for coast watchers warned that ten thousand Japanese were almost unreachable in caves from which their machine guns commanded a clear sweep of the beaches.

It took brave men to jump from landing barges into the surf and under withering fire to go splashing ashore. At every step some of them died. Those who reached the beach often were pinned there in frantically dug foxholes. They could only wait, hoping for deliverance before mortars and machine guns made deliverance too late.

The responsibility of ordering men into such action, facing almost certain death, brought many officers to emotional breakdown. Kolombangara, with its promise of heavy casualties, worried Bill Halsey until his staff suggested a bypassing strategy. Better to seize certain islands and from them block the supplying of others still held by the enemy.

Plans were altered to strike instead at Vella Lavella, thirty-five miles north. On L-day (for " landing ") we put nearly five thousand troops ashore. Seabees went to work to build an airstrip while tough New Zealanders were still probing the jungle, flushing out Japanese. Meanwhile, surprised by our strike at Vella, the enemy were now in a rush to rescue their garrison on Kolombangara before it could be starved out.

Almost nightly barges large enough to carry fifty to a hundred men each put in to Kolombangara, filled and pulled away. Attacked by our watchful PT boats and destroyers, eighteen were chopped up one night, eight another, eleven another, to a total of sixty-two. The Japanese loss must have been more than three thousand men. They abandoned the remainder of their garrison.

The problem of Kolombangara was solved. Vella Lavella cost us a hundred and fifty dead. The island-hopping policy was a success.

[Chapter 15]

# Islands of Lost Japs

AFTER their failure the year before to capture Port Moresby on the southeast coast of New Guinea, the enemy had been steadily shouldered back across that huge island. In early 1943 their last toehold on the part called Papua was lost at the price of sixteen thousand men and an untold number of planes. Only the rusting wrecks of transports and destroyers twitching in the surf were reminders that the Empire of the Rising Sun had been here.

The enemy fell back to the northern Solomons. There our overlapping commands, with MacArthur in strategic charge and Halsey in tactical charge, were squeezing them, island by island, toward the apex of Rabaul.

Bougainville, coded CHERRYBLOSSOM, was next. Torokina on the west coast was its strong point, with supporting airfields at Buka, Bonis, Kahili, Kara, and Ballale. For two weeks a record heavy air bombing and inshore cruiser and destroyer bombardment prepared the way. Beginning soon after midnight of October 31, Buka and nearby Bonis received two thousand four hundred five-inch shells from Admiral Merrill's task force, which then hurried south the length of Bougainville to devote similar attention to Shortlands and Ballale. On L-day, November 1, we attacked on five fronts, some of them two hundred miles apart. Landings were not unduly difficult or costly.

This campaign brought the *Saratoga* into her first combat in more than a year. When the war broke out, she was at San Diego. Speeding to Pearl Harbor, she soon was torpedoed and had to limp back to the mainland and so missed the Battle of Midway. From her lack of combat rose her nickname, "The Model Housing Project."

Twice on L-day the *Sara* threw her planes over Buka-Bonis to finish whatever Merrill's five-inch guns had missed. They shot down twenty-one Zekes besides doing ground damage; the *Sara* had no losses. Then her task force under Admiral Sherman withdrew south of Guadalcanal to refuel and await orders.

Our transports being unloaded at Torokina had to contend with extremely high surf, which upset eighty-six landing craft, and with two heavy air attacks.

Four Japanese cruisers and six destroyers approaching from Rabaul prompted our cargo ships to up-anchor and flee. On L-plus-1 at 0245 Admiral Merrill's four cruisers and eight destroyers stood up to the enemy in a three-hour gun battle that cost the Japanese a cruiser and a destroyer. As Merrill escorted three of his damaged ships southward he was attacked by sixty-five Rabaul bombers. Seventeen were shot down. Our only damage was two hits on the *Montpelier's* catapult. When Merrill's tired crews neared Purvis Bay naval base, a welcoming signal asked, "What do you require?" The answer was, "Sleep."

Now arose what Halsey called the direst emergency of his South Pacific command. It originated on Truk Island, seven hundred miles north of Rabaul. Truk was Japan's greatest air and naval stronghold after her home island of Honshu – so strong that the Allies had yet to bomb it.

Hurrying down from Truk came ten Japanese cruisers and eight destroyers, their obvious intention to seal off Torokina. This would trap our thousands of troops ashore, so that later the enemy could pinch off our other scattered landings. Their success would bring us losses too great to mend and would destroy our Solomons offensive.

Bill Halsey and his staff had flown up from Nouméa to establish advance headquarters on Guadalcanal. At news of the enemy approach, hurriedly they calculated that the Japanese naval force should reach Torokina on L-plus-4. Merrill's task force, our nearest to the challenge, had just begun to load ammunition and fuel. In any case, with three vessels under repair, Merrill's strength was far from enough.

Halsey's only alternative, and a weak one, was to call on Sherman's task force, built around the *Saratoga* and the light carrier *Princeton*. Sherman lay far from Torokina, off the lower end of Guadalcanal, but all his ships were fast and it might be possible, Halsey's staff believed, for a high-speed run to bring him abreast of Torokina in time. They drew up an operation order that specified cruisers as prime targets, destroyers next, and took it to Halsey's Quonset hut for his signature.

As he read it the lines grooved deeper in his face. The Japanese force was far superior in armor to ours. The air groups of both our carriers might well be annihilated. The carriers themselves might be lost. His son was aboard the *Saratoga*. Staring at the wall, Halsey weighed this gamble. His lower jaw thrust out, and to Captain Thurber he growled,

"We can't just stand here wringing our hands while those men on Torokina are wiped out." Seizing a pen, he signed. As he handed back the order he added, "Our only chance is to attack. Attack soon and attack hard."

At thirty knots Sherman's task force raced up the Slot. Assured of air cover from our Bougainville area airfields, he did not need to hold back fighters to protect his ships. As he neared the island he launched every operational plane. Ninety-seven of them passed like a cloud over Bougainville, overwhelmed three Japanese picket planes, and sped on north to meet the enemy force at sea off Rabaul.

Again, as so often before in Halsey's career, sheer audacity helped to make up for inferior strength. P-38's dived like showering arrows while the Japanese were still throwing their full strength of fighters into the air. In the furious twilight battle, twenty-five enemy pilots, considered the finest Japan had, spiraled in flames into the sea. Our cost was five. Our bombers, breaking through the wall of AA, damaged six cruisers and two destroyers.

Darkness halted the battle. The Tokyo Express underwent a change of heart and did not run that night. Next morning only one cruiser and a few destroyers could be found, roosting in Simpson Harbor, Rabaul. The remainder of the Express was scurrying full speed back to Truk.

In the pause, our strength on Bougainville was rapidly built up in men and planes. Meanwhile, the enemy's attempts to cover small craft landings to evacuate pockets of troops triggered air battles with one-sided scores. One clash saw twenty-four Japanese planes shot down to seven of ours; in another, we traded three American planes for fifty of theirs.

Periodically we mounted simultaneous bomber attacks from five airfields to reach up to Rabaul. In a destroyer action, five against five, Captain " 31 Knot " Burke sank three enemy " tin cans " in the murky waters of the Slot and chased the other two all the way to Simpson Harbor. Rabaul's offensive power was being ground finer, though her defenses remained formidable.

Halsey became aware that New Britain, on which Rabaul lay, with New Ireland close by, need not be taken by assault. The geography of the area offered them another chance to leapfrog.

Supporting Rabaul was nearby Kavieng Island. Halsey proposed to MacArthur that he occupy Green Island a hundred twenty miles from Rabaul. Kavieng could similarly be blocked from Emirau, ninety miles distant from it. Manus Island at two hundred twenty miles from Kavieng commanded the western approaches to both Rabaul and Kavieng. It was impossible for the Japanese to control all the dozens of islands, and these three, known to be lightly garrisoned, should be readily overcome.

Military plans for the movement and supply of large forces must be worked out in precise detail weeks and often months in advance. Thus all MacArthur's forces already had been assigned to winning certain objectives at certain times as steps in certain larger coming operations. An abrupt change of plans could throw carefully meshed instructions into endless confusion, which in turn could invite disaster. Thus MacArthur was not able to radio back a simple yes or no to Halsey's suggestion but must, with his staff, consider all aspects of altering long-held plans.

Before SOWESPAC decided, Bill Halsey was summoned to Pearl Harbor to confer with Admiral Nimitz. He flew on to California where, his business completed, for the first time in sixteen months he was able to visit with Mrs. Halsey. The *Saratoga* happened to be in port, and they were joined by their son Bill. Later, Halsey went to Washington, where Secretary of the Navy Knox awarded him a Gold Star in lieu of a second Distinguished Service Medal. In part the citation read:

> A forceful and inspiring leader, Admiral Halsey indoctrinated his command with his own fighting spirit and an invincible determination to destroy the enemy. His daring, initiative, and superb tactical skill have been responsible for the continued success of the South Pacific Campaign and have contributed vitally toward breaking down Japanese resistance.

In his conferences with Admiral King in Washington, Halsey outlined his bypass strategy as to Rabaul. If successful, he declared, it would ring down the curtain on the South Pacific theater. COMINCH approved, subject because of their overlapping authority in the combat area, to General MacArthur's approval. A meeting of the two commanders was arranged at Pearl Harbor, but as matters turned out, neither Halsey nor MacArthur could attend.

Their representatives reached agreement as to which islands should be seized to bypass enemy strongholds with what forces and when. Through misunderstanding or lack of clarity in the agreement, MacArthur, when he studied the result, refused to approve. He felt Manus Island was not suitable for the use Halsey projected for it. Furthermore, Manus lay within SOWESPAC, though COMSOPAC appeared to be assuming authority for it.

In the end Halsey flew to Brisbane to settle the matter. Although the atmosphere between the principals was again cordial, MacArthur at first bluntly rejected Halsey's explanation. Later, Halsey thought he had won him over. But early the next morning Halsey had to repeat his arguments. Again the matter was settled.

But MacArthur called for another conference. Halsey and his aides for the third time presented their arguments in full detail. Once more, keeping his emotions under stern control, MacArthur weighed each statement, asked questions, and offered his own arguments.

He was silent a long moment. Suddenly smiling, he aimed the stem of his corncob pipe at Halsey. "Bill, you are absolutely right." He turned to his aide, General Sutherland. "Dick, we'll go ahead the way the Admiral wants it."

Later, to one of his own aides Halsey marveled, "Any man who can stay as objective as he was through hours of discussion can't help being a great general."

On Bougainville, Choiseul, Shortlands, Treasury, and half a dozen other islands under Allied control there were continual skirmishes with remaining pockets of the enemy. Minor actions in size, they were nevertheless savage, for whatever could be said about a Japanese, he never surrendered. He would fight to the death, and to be captured must be overpowered. He secreted himself in mountain caves where he could be flushed out only by flamethrowers. Or he somehow eked out an existence in the jungle, and concealed in trees, sniped at passing Americans. Some ingenious GI thought of sticking razor blades into tree bark, and this located many a hidden sniper when he descended and burst into yells of pain.

Driven by hunger, Japanese frequently risked the bayonet they so disliked in order to stage brief, furious raids on our supplies. A lone fugitive on Choiseul stole food each evening while an officers' mess was being cleared, then under cover of darkness moved among the soldiers to an outdoor motion-picture show. As, for the fifth evening, he sat watching a Hollywood film the lights suddenly came on. A doctor informed the audience that every man must stand inspection to make sure he wore shoes and socks against chiggers. Military Police guarded all exits. The Japanese, who was barefoot, was discovered.

On Manus Island after its capture a certain area presented special difficulties in mopping up. Something like a game preserve was established, with Japanese for the game. Here new troops could practice scouting and patrolling. Food was left out to keep the quarry in good condition. A " bag limit " of two Japanese per hunter was fixed, but no GI was ever arrested for taking more than his quota.

The losses to the enemy in men abandoned must have reached large figures. On New Britain the First Marines and elements of the Sixth Army under SOWESPAC closed the only overland escape route from Rabaul. This sealed the fate of fifty thousand Japanese. Another thirty thousand on Bougainville and Choiseul kept our troops probing and exterminating for weeks, and there were unknown numbers on other islands.

Guadalcanal, New Georgia, Rendova, Bougainville, New Britain, all with their strong points subdued, had been wrested from the enemy. By March 25, 1944, organized resistance in the Solomon Islands was over.

In mid-June that year, Halsey's wartime career entered its third stage. In the first, he commanded a task force at sea. In the second, for nineteen months he commanded the South Pacific war theater and all the forces within it. In May he had been summoned to San Francisco where, to his delight, King and Nimitz informed him that he was going back to sea in command of the Third Fleet.

[Chapter 16]

# Strategy Change

BEFORE OUR ENTRY into the war even a well-informed industrialist would have doubted the United States' ability to produce in only two years the tremendous flood of arms we attained by 1944. The mightiest industrial nation in history turned almost overnight – the night of December 7, 1941 – from building the products desired in peace to those needed for our defense over a large part of the globe.

Aircraft, previously made in dozens, now rolled off production lines in hundreds every day. Far from any sizable body of water, assault barges, PT boats, and the huge propulsion gears of transports were built. Clothing manufacturers turned exclusively to the needs of twelve million men in uniform, and makers of small mechanical articles changed their machines to produce parts for dozens of wartime needs, from bombsights to flare pistols.

The intricacy of modern war implements did not delay their production. Parts made in Pennsylvania readily fitted others made in Illinois. Five miles of electrical wiring went into a heavy bomber, and on its first flight this dizzying maze responded perfectly to the pilot's fingertip control. Several thousand parts drawn from all sections of the nation were joined, and a destroyer lay ready to cast off her lines. Literally square miles of tanks, trucks, and jeeps rolled by their own power from under factory roofs where they had been born; and in

East Coast, West Coast, and Gulf Coast yards all manner of ships, from seagoing tugs to tankers and battle cruisers, slid down the ways into salt water almost daily.

All this had to be, and it was. We were supplying the needs of half a dozen allies as well as our own forces.

In addition to making the tools of war, we trained the men to wield them — soldiers, sailors, Marines, aircraft crews, officers. By scores of thousands they studied and drilled at more than twelve hundred army camps, naval stations, and air bases scattered about the United States. Accountants were trained to be bayonet-wielding Rangers, college juniors became fighter plane pilots, farm boys learned to navigate an attack transport from Seattle to some tiny atoll five thousand miles away off New Georgia.

It had been in large part our lack of armor that had encouraged the Japanese to attempt to seize domination over millions of Asians, and encouraged Hitler and Mussolini to try to subdue all Europe and North Africa. Two years earlier it had seemed that the dictators might succeed, but by the Battle of Guadalcanal our power was noticeably enlarging. Now in all war theaters the Allies were stronger.

The change can be seen in one example. Two months after the Pearl Harbor raid Halsey's Task Force 8, audaciously striking at Japanese-held Wotje and Maloelap, consisted of the carrier *Enterprise*, three cruisers, and six destroyers.

In June, 1944, Admiral Nimitz turned over to Halsey command of the Third Fleet. Now he had at his disposal a dozen task forces, each treble the strength of his old TF 8. He had nearly thirty light and full-size aircraft carriers. He had dozens of cruisers and nearly two hundred destroyers. With all its auxiliary vessels, Third Fleet totaled over five hundred ships.

It was still, of course, a big war, spread over an immense area. The enemy had got his nose bloodied on New Guinea and again in the Solomons, and he had been forced to pull back. But he still controlled vast reaches of water and land, still had large armies and a powerful navy and air force. He had been thrown off the offensive to the defensive, but defensive usually costs fewer lives.

Exactly what the next Allied campaign should be was a complex problem. Choices had to be made among a score of targets. MacArthur and Admiral King suggested a strike at Formosa or Japan. Halsey objected that Formosa would be difficult to subdue and was not of immediate strategic importance. He and Nimitz favored striking directly at the Philippines.

In the light of the latest information and by change and compromise a plan was worked out. It was to be applied in two phases, leading up to Halsey, Nimitz, and MacArthur's preferred target, the Philippines.

At times the Third Fleet was divided for operational needs into Third and Fifth. Admiral Spruance commanded the Fifth. Halsey retained overall command and when the two parts joined, the common title was Third. The off-and-on use of "Third" and "Fifth" confused enemy Intelligence, which at times believed we had twice as much armor as we had.

Phase One, scheduled for mid-September, 1944, called for capture of Angaur and Peleliu islands. Phase Two in early October listed Yap and Ulithi. They were to the northeast of the Palau group. These would be amphibious landings, combining warships, transports for Army and Marine invaders, cargo ships carrying supplies, and hundreds of assault craft, with air cover for all. Despite the frequency with which Allied forces made amphibious landings on Pacific islands, they were among the most complicated and hazardous of all operations. Halsey's staff with the staffs of Amphibious Forces Admiral Wilkinson and Marine General Geiger, labored six weeks to thresh out the details of the two phases.

In late June, Admiral Spruance, with the Fifth Fleet, fought the important Philippine Sea battle, then attacked Guam and Saipan, the Volcano Islands, and the Ryukyu Islands. Badly in need of rest, Admiral Spruance was relieved in August. The

Fifth Fleet now melted into the Third.

Mitscher sent three task forces against the Palaus and a fourth against Yap, and soon made two strikes against Mindanao, the southernmost large Philippine island. When he reported the Army's Fifth Air Force had completed wrecking enemy resistance on Mindanao, Halsey signaled him for a meeting at sea. It was decided to move on at once to attack the Central Philippines.

Bill Halsey was glad to be once more on shipboard. Life seemed somehow freer than when he had been figuratively chained to maps and desks as COMSOPAC on Nouméa. He called shipboard " the land of whistles " because, though boatswains' pipes seldom penetrated flag plot, they were heard in every other cranny of every Navy vessel fifty to eighty times a day.

Life afloat was directed by gongs, bugles, and whistles. The gongs clattered for General Quarters or to announce a high ranking officer coming aboard. Bugles sounded Air Alert and various lesser messages. Scarcely a quarter hour passed, night or day, without the querulous *Pheeep* of the pencil-thin silver bosun's pipe followed by his singsong, " Now hear this," followed by some announcement.

Dawn was greeted with *Pheeep.* " Now hear this. Sunrise! Light ship! " The day ended officially, according to latitude and season, with: " Now hear this. Darken ship. The smoking lamp is out on all weather decks." During daylight hours the calls came spasmodically, and every man learned to maintain half-attention in case the current announcement affected him.

*Pheeep.* " Now hear this. Turn to! All sweepers man your brooms. Clean sweepdown, fore and aft! "

Or: " Extra-duty men lay down to the master-at-arms! "

*Pheeep.* " Now hear this. The smoking lamp is out throughout the ship while taking aboard aviation gas and fuel oil."

*Pheeep.* " Relieve the watch! "

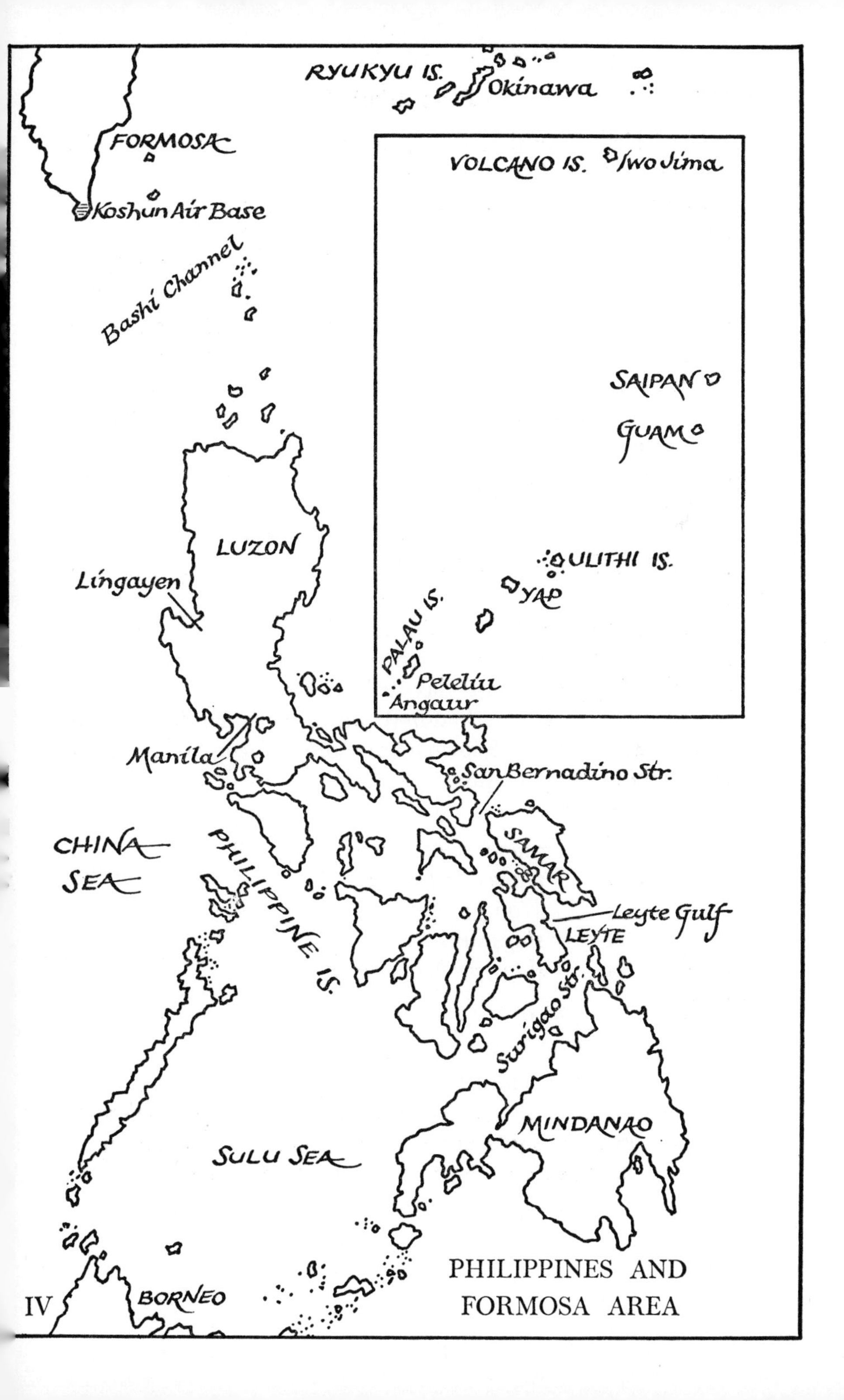


IV

PHILIPPINES AND FORMOSA AREA

Or: " Now hear this. Religious services on the after flight deck have the following schedule."

*Pheeep.* " Aviation mechs assemble hangar deck aft. It's a lecture."

Sometimes the bosun's peculiar high squeal blew Air Alert. " Bogeys on the horizon. On the double to your stations! " Always after the gongs hammered throughout the ship the *Pheeep* added his urging. " General Quarters! General Quarters! All hands man battle stations. On the double! "

One deck officer was said to have become weary of the bosun's constant piping and chatter — mostly, he declared, about trivialities. He requested the chief bosun to call a *Pheeep* to end all *Pheeeps.*

" Put this on the PA," he suggested. " ' Now hear this. All men who have not already done so, do so immediately. On the double! '

" That," he declared with satisfaction, " ought to start sixteen hundred confused sailors rushing somewhere or other."

In the Third Fleet's first-day strike at the Central Philippines her airmen flew twelve hundred sorties, with another twelve hundred the next day. Shown a box score of the operation, Halsey gave a low exclamation.

| Japanese | | United States |
|---|---|---|
| 173 | *planes shot down* | 8 |
| 305 | *planes destroyed on ground* | 0 |
| 59 | *ships sunk* | 0 |
| 58 | *ships probably sunk* | 0 |

All this at a cost of ten Americans.

From: COMTHIRDFLEET
To: Carriers, Third Fleet

BECAUSE OF BRILLIANT PERFORMANCE MY GROUP OF STARS HAS JUST GIVEN, I AM BOOKING YOU TO APPEAR BEFORE BEST AUDIENCE IN ASIATIC THEATER

By " best " Halsey meant the Japanese in their chief Philippine stronghold, Manila.

In planning Third Fleet's operations the principle of flexibility had been kept uppermost so that advantage could be seized of any unexpected favorable development. Halsey's strikes at Mindanao and the Central Philippines turned up just such a favorable development – the fact that these areas were poorly defended. This hinted that Manila itself might be ripe for assault, at the same time mounting a far larger offensive to include other points in the islands.

Bringing his thoughts to sharper focus, Halsey believed it now was needless for MacArthur to commence his Philippines invasion on Mindanao. That was hundreds of miles from the final key target, Manila. Mindanao could be left to wither if Leyte, the next island north, were invaded instead. The change of plan should bring about a considerable saving in lives and time.

Pacing the bridge of the *New Jersey,* now his flagship, Halsey considered and reconsidered. It was no small thing to suggest an abrupt switch in grand strategy once arrangements were firmly laid to move thousands of troops and hundreds of ships on precise schedules. Possibilities for mix-ups and confusion were enormous. If the enemy took advantage of such confusion, our losses could be staggering.

Offsetting this risk was the possibility of shortening the war.

Bill Halsey huddled alone in a corner of his bridge. Once more he carefully thought through the suggestion that had come to him. Shoulders squared, he marched into flag plot and calling his staff together, laid his proposal before them. They evaluated combat reports, Intelligence data, and the availability of MacArthur's forces. To a man they voted, " Admiral, it's a sound idea."

His dispatch to CINCPAC recommended that seizure of Yap and the Palaus be abandoned; that the assault troops thus released be added to MacArthur's invasion force; and that landings on Leyte instead of Mindanao be undertaken at the earliest possible date.

CINCPAC replied in an hour that Phase One of the Western Carolines operations must be carried through. Halsey's other suggestions were being forwarded, however, to COMINCH and SOWESPAC. It so happened that at this time President Roosevelt, Prime Minister Churchill, and the Allied Joint Chiefs of Staff were in conference at Quebec. The American Joint Chiefs withdrew from a dinner to assess Halsey's suggestions. Within ninety minutes the signal reached Admiral Nimitz at Pearl Harbor and General MacArthur in Australia to abandon the previously approved landings and to execute the Leyte operation on October 20 instead, two full months ahead of schedule.

In September the islands of Peleliu, Angaur, and Ulithi were captured, but the price to us was eight thousand men killed, wounded, or missing. The Japanese lost twelve thousand. We gained two harbors and one airstrip.

Now the mighty Third Fleet stood northwestward for an attack on Manila. Launching from a hundred fifty miles, the Americans achieved clear surprise. No Japanese fighter plane took the air in defense for ten minutes; in fact, from a Manila dock a Japanese officer pointed to the invaders and boasted: "See our splendid war eagles. How smoothly they maneuver!" Then the bombs began to fall. In a one-day strike ended by bad weather, Mitscher reported four hundred five planes destroyed, or damaged, a hundred three ships sunk or damaged, and both Clark and Nichols fields gutted. Meanwhile, the total cost to our forces was fifteen planes and a dozen men lost, but no ship touched.

After a day spent refueling, the carriers made a high-speed run for Coron Bay in the belief that it would be crowded with ships that had fled from Manila. It was. From three hundred fifty miles the carriers launched, and their planes rolled up the score of five tankers, one transport and thirteen cargo ships, one destroyer and three destroyer escorts sunk, and fifty-three others, many small, damaged. The three weeks' total for the Third Fleet was one thousand five aircraft destroyed and a hundred fifty-three ships sunk, not counting small harbor craft that were lost.

After a month at sea the Third hoped for a week's rest at anchor at Ulithi but a typhoon drove the ships from the harbor to ride out the storm. A few days later the task began of running interference for MacArthur's landing on Leyte. The Fleet had already cut down enemy air strength in the Philippines and now sought to wreck enemy bases from which this strength could be replenished. These were widely scattered, from Marcus Island to Formosa and north to south in the sprinkling of small islands off Japan from Amami O Shima to Myako Jima. Success attended these efforts, with small losses to us but large losses to the enemy. In drawing away from Formosa the heavy cruiser *Canberra* (replacing one sunk earlier) was torpedoed and lay dead in the water.

She was taken in tow by the *Wichita*, with the prospect of a thirteen-hundred-mile trip to Ulithi at four knots an hour. In a vicious air attack the accompanying cruiser *Houston* (also replacing a cruiser sunk earlier) was torpedoed, her engine room flooded. Debating the possible cost of now defending two cripples, Halsey decided to use them as bait for a large naval engagement. He named Admiral Wiltse COMBAITDIV and sent task forces just over the horizon in several directions. Then he waited, hoping the enemy would strike. But their reconnaissance evidently perceived the trap, for no sizable force appeared.

Their pace slowed to three and a half knots, the *Canberra* and *Houston*, both listing, made their long, crabbed voyage to port and lived to fight again.

President Roosevelt sent a personal message to the Third Fleet:

> It is with pride that the country has followed your fleet's magnificent sweep into enemy waters x In addition to the gallant fighting of your fliers we appreciate the endurance and superseamanship of your forces

Halsey would have liked to rest his Fleet, but there was no rest. A battle waited, and the Third Fleet sailed to meet it.

[Chapter 17]

# Task Force 34

TO THE JAPANESE it was known as the Second Battle of the Philippine Sea. Americans called it the Battle for Leyte Gulf. The purpose each side had in the action determined the choice of name.

The enemy intention was to lure a large part of our naval power to open sea, and while engaging it there, to smash the remainder left guarding General MacArthur's October 20 troop landing on Leyte. The American purpose was to build up that foothold on Leyte as a start toward recapturing the Philippines and to cripple the Japanese navy so it could not pour more defenders into the islands.

To beat back our attempt at reoccupation, the enemy plan, coded *Sho*-1, had been ready for months. When Supreme Commander of the Imperial Navy Admiral Oikawa became convinced that MacArthur had made good his landing on Leyte, he sent the order crackling over the Pacific to units of the Japanese fleet:

SHO-1 OPERATION ALERT — EXECUTE

This classic battle conception was the work of Fleet Admiral Toyoda, considered Japan's keenest naval tactician and a man who studied the personalities of his opponents as much as he studied the armor they commanded. Toyoda saw General MacArthur as the bulldog type who would fight to the end to hold any landing he made. He knew Bill Halsey's rocklike belief that the best defense always was offense. Toyoda's plan was shaped to take cunning advantage of both men's fundamental traits.

Our forces afloat were under two separate commands. This violated an age-old military principle and claimed its cost. The Seventh Fleet, commanded by Admiral Kinkaid, was under General MacArthur's control. Defensive in makeup, the Seventh's light aircraft carriers, old battleships, cruisers, and destroyers had convoyed MacArthur's transports to Leyte, provided a bombardment to cover their landing, and now protected the buildup of their supplies.

The Third Fleet under Halsey, and in turn under CINCPAC, was offensive in character. Its fast new battleships and carriers roved the ocean, searching for an enemy to fight. Its principal attack unit was Admiral Mitscher's Task Force 38, which in turn was made up of Task Groups 38.1, 38.2, 38.3, and 38.4 commanded by Admirals McCain, Bogan, Sherman, and Davison. Each task group of about twenty-three ships was built around two large and two light aircraft carriers.

It is a footnote to record that Halsey's flagship, the new battleship *New Jersey*, was part of Bogan's group. Mitscher's flagship was the carrier *Lexington* in Sherman's.

Admiral Toyoda reasoned that however many task groups he sent toward the Philippines, Halsey would not identify any as the main striking force unless it included aircraft carriers. So Toyoda's strategy was to send three moderate-size task groups which, at the right time, would converge on the Seventh Fleet and our troops on Leyte. Meanwhile, far distant, he would show Halsey a carrier group. Halsey would believe this the main striking force and in rushing out to meet it, be drawn too far away to help the Seventh. The upshot, Toyoda believed, would be annihilation of the Seventh Fleet and MacArthur's troops, and Halsey would have fought a sea battle of no great importance.

None of this was suspected by the Americans. From their

viewpoint the beginning of the complicated battle was our submarine *Darter's* signal on October 23 that enemy warships were nearing the southwest tip of the Philippines. Inasmuch as the main Japanese naval strength was based these days at Singapore and in Borneo, the *Darter's* information seemed to hint some major movement under way.

Of Third Fleet's four task groups, McCain's was en route to Ulithi for rest and supply. The other three were in waters east of the Philippines. Halsey ordered the three to throw out aircraft searches to cover the island chain's whole western coast. Sifting the reports the pilots sent in on the twenty-fourth, he saw that the Japanese were bringing up three battle groups. One came from the south, another from the southwest, the third from the northwest. None included aircraft carriers.

As the hours passed he strove to guess what the Japanese were up to. Where were their carriers?

He ordered Sherman and Davison to draw nearer Bogan so the three task groups would be some hundred miles apart about midway along the east side of the Philippine chain. He called on McCain to reverse his Ulithi course, refuel at sea, and be ready for any need that developed.

Bogan's scouts reported at 0820 the advance of the Central Force. His Task Group 38.2 planes, reaching out, sank the enemy's newest and largest battleship *Musashi,* three cruisers, and a destroyer. The enemy withdrew in confusion to the west. then turned and came back by direct order of Toyoda in Japan: " Trusting in Divine Assistance, all forces will advance to the attack."

At 0943, Davison sighted the Southern Force, but because Seventh Fleet was nearby and possessed three times the armor of Southern, he did not attack; instead, he went to Bogan's aid against the Central Force.

Sherman's TG 38.3 was under violent attack by land-based planes from Luzon. Although a hundred and ten of the enemy were shot down, some wormed through the AA to bomb the light carrier *Princeton.* Hastily taking off her crew, Sherman ordered her sunk – our first carrier loss since the *Hornet* at Santa Cruz two years before.

With the enemy intention still not fully clear, Halsey at 1510 sent a dispatch to all Third Fleet task group commanders outlining a tactic he *might* decide to use. If a surface engagement seemed likely at San Bernadino Strait, he might carve out and make operative under Vice Admiral Lee, Task Force 34, comprising uncommitted battleships, cruisers, and destroyers. This message was mistakenly accepted by Seventh Fleet, for whom it was not intended. Its misinterpretation by Rear Admiral Kinkaid probably cost Admiral Toyoda the success of his imaginative plan.

At 1730 on the twenty-fourth, Sherman's planes found the answer to Halsey's question: Where were the enemy carriers?

The fourth Japanese force was sighted approaching the Philippines from a completely opposite point of the compass, the northeast. It numbered a large carrier, three light carriers, two old battleships converted to carriers, cruisers, and destroyers. This was Toyoda's bait to lure Halsey far eastward of the Philippines. This, Halsey believed, was the main striking force, the one he must deal with.

Peculiarly, the Japanese carrier group and those other three forces west of the islands all advanced at a leisurely fifteen knots. Their common speed hinted a meeting planned. Such a meeting might be intended off Samar Island, where they could wheel and in unison attack our transports unloading at Leyte.

Kinkaid's Seventh Fleet appeared capable of handling its assignment of safeguarding our troops on Leyte. Free to operate on the offensive, Halsey had three choices for disposing his armor:

1. To collect his entire Third Fleet at San Bernadino Strait between Samar and Luzon, and wait to meet the enemy.

2. To guard San Bernadino with a task group and strike at the Japanese Northern Force with his carriers.

3. To leave San Bernadino unguarded and strike with his whole fleet at the Japanese Northern Force.

Pacing his flag bridge, he considered these alternatives. Deciding, Halsey went into flag plot and touched his finger on the Northern Force's charted position three hundred miles away. To Admiral Carney he said: "Here's where we're going. Start them north."

The hour was 1950. Carney began to scribble dispatches to McCain and Sherman to join Bogan and Davison, course 000 (due north), speed twenty-five knots. He informed Seventh Fleet of the move and added for their use the estimate of 38.2's fliers: "Central Force heavily damaged." Kinkaid soon learned this was an exaggeration.

At dawn on the twenty-fifth, air patrols established the exact composition of the oncoming enemy carrier force, which was in two units, forty miles apart. Task group commanders prepared their first aerial strikes at 0630. Then Wildcats and Avengers took off and winged away to the northeast. Now aboard the Third Fleet ships began the anxious wait for news of their success.

An hour and a half passed. Two hours. At 0850 came the report:

ONE CARRIER SUNK AFTER TREMENDOUS EXPLOSION X TWO CARRIERS, ONE LIGHT CRUISER HIT BADLY X OTHER CARRIER UNTOUCHED X FORCE COURSE 150 SPEED 17

The Third's groups increased their speed. If the enemy held his course, by noon there would be a ship-to-ship big-gun battle. Halsey rubbed his hands in anticipation of blasting out of the water the Japanese vessels already crippled by our planes.

A dispatch, at 0648, from Seventh Fleet had puzzled him: "Am now engaging enemy surface forces Surigao Strait x Question is 34 guarding San Bernadino Strait." He replied: "Negative." What did Kinkaid care about the mythical 34? He added, "It is with our carriers now engaging enemy carriers."

The Japanese Southern Force pushing into Surigao Strait late on the night of the twenty-fourth gave Seventh's task force under Rear Admiral Oldendorf every naval officer's dream opportunity. Oldendorf had thirty-nine PT boats guarding the strait's southern approaches, three destroyer squadrons near its center, and at the mouth to Leyte Gulf his battleships and cruisers.

About 1100 hours PT boat radars picked up the oncoming enemy and the PT's attacked in waves. Next, destroyers rushed in. In turn the battleships opened murderous fire and in minutes the enemy toll was two battleships and three destroyers sunk. Later Oldendorf's planes sank a heavy and a light cruiser. His loss was one PT boat sunk and one destroyer damaged.

That morning at 0830, Halsey, miles to the northeast, received another dispatch from Kinkaid: " Urgently need fast battleships Leyte Gulf at once." Trying to understand this, Halsey watched the second aerial strike take off from his task force. He hurried into flag plot to study the chart. He was pulling away from that distant area where the Seventh was operating; what could he do to help? He ordered McCain's task group fueling at sea: " Strike enemy vicinity 11-20 N 127-00 E at best possible speed " and notified Kinkaid this assistance was on the way.

At 0900 came a stronger appeal: " Cover Leyte top speed x Request fast carriers make immediate strike." But Halsey, with his forces already committed, could do nothing about this except grow more indignant at the obvious foulup. What had gone wrong with the Seventh? They had their responsibility; he had his. In a few minutes still another message read: " Request immediate air strike x Also request support by heavy ships x My battleships low on ammunition."

Low on ammunition? For battlewagons, whose heavy guns were their chief asset, to be in need of ammunition at a crucial time was astonishing. Scanning the series of messages, Halsey noticed that some had been unaccountably delayed in transit. He stared at them, trying to envision the sequence of events in Seventh Fleet's area.

A new dispatch was handed to him:

From: CINCPAC
To: COMTHIRDFLEET
THE WHOLE WORLD WANTS TO KNOW WHERE IS TASK FORCE 34

Bill Halsey was stunned. This from Pearl Harbor?

Wordless, he thrust the paper at Admiral Carney to read. Now even Admiral Nimitz was demanding to know the whereabouts of Task Force 34 — *and there was none.* Could Nimitz think Bill Halsey would form such a force without notifying CINCPAC? Gaining their approval? That he carried on his command in a deceitful way?

Deeply insulted, Bill Halsey at that moment seemed to feel his forty-two years of honorable service in the United States Navy crumbling into dust. *The whole world wants to know* . . . The phrase flashed again and again, like an electric sign, through his brain. His anger erupted as it never had before even at the enemy he hated. Halsey jerked off his cap and hurled it to the deck. He yelled imprecations and jumped on the cap as if to grind the tiny four silver stars under his heel.

Admiral Mick Carney rushed over. "Bill! Stop this! Pull yourself together!"

Halsey quieted. He stood red-faced and ashamed. Composed as quickly as he had given vent to his rage, he took back the dispatch in both trembling hands and reread it. There had to be some explanation. Chester Nimitz, his intimate friend and idolized superior officer, knew Halsey too well, prized him too much, to have used such a phrase: "The whole world wants to know —"

"Here, Bill, settle down." Carney handed him a cup of steaming coffee. "That phrase —" He probed for some explanation. "Chances are it's just dispatcher padding. You know how they throw extra words into dispatches so if the Nips intercept, they'll get the wrong meaning? It was a poor choice of padding," Carney acknowledged, " but that's all it was – only padding."

Sipping his coffee, Halsey eyed him. Carney's explanation might well be correct. Yes, probably it was.

" But we still have to account for Task Force 34," Halsey snapped. " Here we are, engaged with the enemy and hurting him. But the Seventh is in trouble. Let's look at the chart."

Together they studied the symbols showing the last-known locations of the Seventh Fleet and the three enemy diversionary forces that had approached the Philippines from the west. They noted their own position northeast of the islands, closing the enemy carrier force under fierce attack by our planes.

Still simmering, Halsey was reluctant to give up his current engagement. But with the Seventh Fleet in obvious need of assistance from Task Force 34 . . .

Victory was almost within his grasp, and he hesitated another moment. Then he rattled off several orders. Carney watched him with quiet understanding of the decision's cost, and Halsey's aides listened and stared, their mouths open.

The *New Jersey*'s flag log entries for the forenoon watch that October 25 told succinctly the story of Bill Halsey's pursuit of the Japanese, then his reversal.

> *0835 changed speed to 25 knots to close enemy.*
> *0919 course changed to 000 (due north).*
> *1115 course changed to 180 (due south).*

He was deliberately turning away from his quarry. The two remaining carriers of the Northern Force lay dead in the water only forty-two miles from the muzzles of the *New Jersey*'s sixteen-inch rifles which, a few miles closer, could easily sink them. He was leaving what, for him, would have been the biggest naval battle of the war – pulling back to start what later was dubbed " Bull's Run."

His dispatch to Kinkaid read: " TG 38.2 plus six fast battleships proceeding Leyte but unable arrive before 0800 tomorrow."

While 38.2 rushed southward Sherman and Davison's task groups and a swarm of submarines continued on to lambast the Japanese Northern Force. Its total loss was four carriers, one cruiser, and two destroyers sunk, with two battleships, two cruisers, and four destroyers damaged. Curiously, the expected duel of planes from opposing carriers did not come off. Only a handful were on enemy carrier decks and only fifteen in the air. The remainder had flown to Luzon for some purpose unknown and could not get back aboard their carriers to rearm.

By sending the fast new battleships *New Jersey* and *Iowa* ahead with a screen of light cruisers and destroyers while the remainder of two battle groups refueled at sea, Halsey sought to support the Seventh Fleet by intercepting the enemy at 0100 on the twenty-sixth off San Bernadino Strait. Actually, by that hour the Seventh's great struggle of older ships against modern ones was ending. Admiral Sprague's task unit of the Seventh Fleet had taken a severe mauling from the superior Japanese Central Force. Three of Sprague's destroyers charging to within seven thousand yards of enemy battleships had promptly been sunk. Our carrier *Gambier Bay* was lost. The light carrier *Suwannee* in another Seventh task unit was blown apart by enemy suicide planes, and the *Santee* by torpedoes. The enemy's shore-based planes provided them an extra margin of strength.

But the arrival of Task Group 38.1 wrenched the offensive from enemy hands as McCain's fliers swarmed into combat. We still had losses. The *Saint Lo,* afire in a dozen places, had to be abandoned, and the *Kitkun Bay* and *Kalinin Bay,* light carriers, were damaged. By late afternoon the Japanese Central Force was heading full speed for San Bernadino Strait to turn westward and get away, and at dawn of the twenty-sixth McCain and Bogan's planes harried their scattered remnants until bad weather closed in.

Scores of shipwrecked Japanese seamen bobbed in the waters of the Strait, but as usual most preferred joining their ancestors to capture. Only six permitted themselves to be fished out by destroyers.

In the three-day Battle for Leyte Gulf the cost to us was six ships sunk, eleven damaged. Twenty-six enemy ships were sunk and twenty-five damaged. In his official report Halsey gave as results of the battle: (1) failure of the Japanese plan to prevent reoccupation of the Philippines; (2) crushing defeat of the Japanese fleet; (3) elimination of serious naval threat to our operations for many months, if not forever.

COMINCH accepted his first claim but was reluctant to endorse the second and third. However, on October 29 COMINCH did agree and signaled both the Third and Seventh Fleets:

A LARGE PART OF THE ENEMY NAVY HAS BEEN EFFECTUALLY DISPOSED OF FOREVER AND THE REMAINDER FOR SOME TIME TO COME X ALL OFFICERS AND MEN OF YOUR FLEETS HAVE THE HEARTIEST ADMIRATION OF ALL HANDS X WELL DONE

Our division of naval strength into two fleets under separate high commands was, in Halsey's opinion, " an invitation to disaster." Admiral Toyoda, the Japanese tactician, tried to accept that invitation. But United States Navy indoctrination, which made its commanders think strategically alike, caused Toyoda somewhere to fumble.

[Chapter 18]

# The Divine Winds

EVEN IN THE FACE of their staggering naval defeat the enemy refused to concede that Leyte was lost. They began at once to pour new air squadrons into fields on Luzon and Mindanao, and sent troopships threading inner waterways among the seven thousand Philippine islands to new positions blocking MacArthur's progress. His land-based Fifth Air Force proved unable to check the Japanese and because of the rainy season, could not build needed additional airfields. Seventh Fleet air cover could not add enough strength, and MacArthur called for assistance from Task Force 38 carriers.

To provide offshore support meant Halsey must delay resting his battle-weary crews and postpone plans for a strike against the Japanese home islands. His first consideration was for his crews. In three months the *New Jersey* had steamed thirty-six thousand miles. From standing frequent General Alarms and Air Alerts that often continued for hours, the men were worn with fatigue. On the carriers the aircraft accident rate rose steeply until the *Wasp's* flight surgeon pronounced a hundred of her hundred thirty-one pilots physically unfit for more flying.

In this dilemma Halsey sent McCain's and Sherman's task groups to Ulithi for two weeks' rest. To meet MacArthur's need, he ordered Davison's group to cruise off Samar, and Bogan's, including Halsey's flagship, to move northward off Luzon.

There at noon October 29 they learned about *kamikazes*.

The carrier *Intrepid*, which flew Bogan's task group flag, was considered the Navy's unluckiest ship. She had a history of mishaps that put her in drydock so often that she was nicknamed "The Dry I." Now, in an attack by Japanese planes, her patrols shot down twenty-one and AA fire another. But one Japanese pilot bored through the defense and crashed on the *Intrepid* killing six men.

In previous battles crippled Japanese planes had struck our ships, and more than one American pilot, perhaps wounded, his plane out of control, smashed into Japanese vessels. But the way the *Intrepid* had been hit signified a new, purposeful collision technique.

Intelligence had warned sometime ago of "The Divine Wind Special Attack Corps" being organized in Japan, with its pilot members honor-bound to commit suicide. Many of our officers dismissed this as a propaganda threat, "a paper tiger." Americans, they were aware, fight to live and they could not believe that others might fight to die. How many recruits, skeptics inquired, could such a corps attract?

The next day *kamikazes* dived into the carriers *Franklin* and *Belleau Wood*, killing a hundred fifty-eight men, destroying forty-five planes, and forcing both ships out of action. The following day *kamikazes* sank one Seventh Fleet destroyer and damaged five others. In a few more days one enemy flier barely missed crashing on the *Ticonderoga*'s flight deck and splashed into the sea, but a companion spattered himself and his plane against the *Lexington*'s signal bridge, killing forty-six men.

Two weeks later in an action in support of Leyte the *Essex* received a *kamikaze* hit that killed fourteen men and set her afire. She was able to stay in the fight. The *Cabot* lost thirty-four men when a Zeke dived headfirst into her forward deck. The *Intrepid*, struck by her second *kamikaze*, suffered explosions that ruptured gasoline tanks. As the fuel ran down her sides it ignited. Oily smoke rising several thousand feet all but hid her, yet with remarkable seamanship the men on her bridge held her bearing, speed, and position in formation, which undoubtedly prevented collisions. But she lost sixty-nine men, killed or missing, and seventeen planes, and had to creep off to Pearl Harbor.

The Divine Winds, it was painfully obvious, were far more than a paper tiger.

Carriers were prime *kamikaze* targets because of their thin armor, light fire power, and their huge tanks of highly flammable gasoline. To tear up a flight deck or jam an elevator could keep a hundred aircraft out of action. To combat the onslaughts, AA fire was increased and more patrol planes were flown in a wider circle of defense. Still *kamikazes* came hurtling out of the skies.

Although the planes themselves were expendable, how long could Japan continue this waste of pilots? It was known that her finest had long since been decimated, and recent combat showed steady deterioration in the quality of enemy fliers. The *kamikazes* suggested a desperation use of men who, before the war or in its early stages, would have been washed out of training. Now they were accepted, taught the rudiments, pumped full of fervor to die for the Emperor and sent on their one-way rides.

The *kamikaze* menace was deadly. The bravest man could not help feeling terror when he found himself standing on a carrier's deck where a screaming, power-diving Zeke or Jake fighter plane meant to splash itself. Pilots in waiting planes, mechanics servicing them, flight-deck control men, AA gunners in their perches, and even personnel on the bridge were in rife danger. Our losses were heavy in men and costly in ship damage. The *kamikaze* threat had to be overcome.

Carefully gathered statistics showed that of every hundred *kamikaze* attempts, only one plane broke through our defenses and succeeded in doing the damage intended. Others were shot down or missed their marks and plunged into the sea. Thus our record was good, yet that 1 percent of enemy successes claimed fearful cost.

The problem of improving defense fell into three parts: short-, medium-, and long-range.

Short-range defense was AA. There was no way to improve it except to give our gunners more practice. As to medium-range, it was found that some *kamikaze* pilots trailed our planes home and with them slipped past our identification radar. Or by diving from twelve o'clock, straight overhead, or coming in low over the water they evaded probing radar beams. As countermoves, Halsey stationed picket destroyers well away from the main force and ordered homing planes to circle them in specific ways for identification. He stationed " Jack " fighters to patrol low over the water to intercept *kamikazes* before they could start their runs.

For improved long-range defense, our newly trained night fighter pilots were invaluable. Now carrier patrols could be flown twenty-four hours a day. Enemy airfields could be pounded at any hour and were given special attention just before dawn to discourage flights taking off.

None of these improvements was thought of or put into effect in a day. The *kamikaze* menace was dealt with by trial and error and meanwhile represented a strain on nerves and drain on personnel and equipment. For the Japanese, the mad technique gave lessening results, although they continued using *kamikaze* attacks to the end of the war.

Davison's and Bogan's task groups got their turn at rest on Ulithi, and Halsey with them. For months at sea his day had begun at 0500 to watch the first air strikes take off. It did not end until 2400. The nineteen hours between were filled with staff conferences, decisions, planning, and sheer worrying, and often as not his precious five hours' sleep was interrupted. The two weeks ashore were not enough for him mentally and physically to " unwind," but at least they did provide some feeling of renewal.

The middle of December the fleet supported MacArthur's invasion of Mindoro, its task to neutralize enemy airfields on that island. The Third performed with marked success, sinking thirty-three ships and destroying two hundred seventy planes at a cost of only twenty-seven of ours. Not one bandit (enemy plane) was permitted closer to the carriers than twenty miles.

Later that month the fleet was to provide aerial cover for MacArthur's next move, the advance on Luzon, but it was struck by its greatest disaster of the war. The blow came, not from the Japanese but from nature in the form of a great typhoon. Wind velocity reached ninety-three knots. Waves seventy feet high slapped at vessels from all directions at once. Sheets of rain and scud whipped horizontally by the wind made it impossible to distinguish the ocean from the air. From the *New Jersey*'s flag bridge Halsey could not see her bow. Her massive forty-five thousand tons, decks continually awash, were flung about like a block of wood.

Aboard smaller vessels life was completely miserable and often hung by a thread. Badly needed refueling operations had to be abandoned when the wind snapped hoses and threatened to bash ships together. Some destroyers began the four-day blow with only 10 percent of their needs.

Any man swept overboard was impossible to help, and life rafts and small boats were smashed or washed away. Scores of arms and legs were broken as bucking ships flung men down companionways or against steel bulkheads. When the wind heeled over a destroyer until her stack almost scooped water, no one without a firm hold could stay aboard and all hands prayed during tense seconds that she would bob back upright. Meanwhile, ocean water shorting circuits killed electrical power, steering, lights, and communications, and aboard the *Hickox* even knocked out a boiler by salting.

Nature's war on the United States Navy cost seven hundred ninety men lost, the destroyers *Spence, Hull,* and *Monoghan* swamped and sunk, two hundred planes smashed, and twenty-eight ships damaged, nine so severely that they had to be detached for repairs.

The day before Christmas, Admiral Nimitz was piped aboard the *New Jersey* with appropriate honors for his newly won fifth star. He brought a Christmas tree to raise war-weary morale, although Halsey declared that even if Santa Claus were seen descending one of the *New Jersey*'s enormous stacks, he doubted it would rouse real holiday spirit. Halsey himself was having his fourth Christmas away from home because of the war.

"Peace on earth," he agreed, "is decidedly what every man of us longs for."

Permitting the enemy no pause, early in January, 1945, the Americans, for the first time except by submarine, dared to invade the China Sea. Halsey led the Third Fleet, including Task Force 38, in a series of strikes at Formosa. No strong resistance was encountered, indicating that the enemy had weakened their inner defense armor to strengthen outlying bastions. Only bad weather kept the Third's tally down to a hundred eleven planes destroyed and sixteen ships sunk. The next assignment was to share coverage with Seventh Fleet of MacArthur's Lingayen Gulf landing. This was Halsey's final action in the Philippines.

Steaming back to Formosa, the Third struck again to distract from MacArthur's land movements and that night headed boldly south across the China Sea. The passage through Bashi Channel was only eighty miles from the large Japanese air base of Koshun, a risk for American warships that would have been suicidal three years earlier. Now Japan was losing the war, and her people were beginning to know it.

Our progress at Lingayen Gulf evidently made local enemy air force commanders forget to maintain patrols, for only three transport planes were sighted. Our night fighters shot them down. Their loss made Tokyo radio almost hysterical, and our code experts learned the planes had carried the fleeing operations staff of the Philippine Air Command—proof that militarily the Japanese were now abandoning the Philippines.

Raiding Camranh Bay netted forty-one ships sunk and twenty-eight damaged. An obliging monsoon blew some of the damaged vessels ashore, but did not harm the Third. Later TF 38 sank the captured French cruiser *Lamotte-Picquet* at Saigon and the Japanese cruiser *Kashii* at sea. The operation established that the hitherto untouchable inner supply route from Singapore, Burma, Borneo, and the Dutch East Indies to the Japanese home islands was shattered.

In traversing thirty-eight hundred miles of South China Sea, not one of our ships suffered battle damage, but this good fortune ended at our last quick strike at Formosa. The carrier *Langley* lost one man and suffered bomb damage. Two *kamikazes* dived headlong into the *Ticonderoga,* killing a hundred forty men and smashing her island structure, flight deck, and hangar deck. Another *kamikaze* hit the destroyer *Maddox,* killing four men.

For the Third Fleet, there followed a wait off Okinawa while photographic planes mapped the part of the island of special strategic importance to our later amphibious landing there. On January 26, Halsey, with vast relief, turned over his command to Admiral Spruance.

In five months at sea the Third had destroyed seven thousand three hundred fifteen planes. It had sunk ninety warships and five hundred seventy-three merchant vessels. In a heartfelt farewell dispatch Halsey told all hands of his command:

> NO WORDS CAN EXPRESS MY PRIDE X SUPERLATIVELY WELL DONE

The happy prospect of a visit with his family in the States was somewhat clouded for Bill Halsey as the moment neared for actual parting. Perhaps never again would he be associated with all these thousands of splendid young Americans. The thought brought a lump in his throat. Watching his personal belongings being packed, he struggled against a sense of deepening gloom – until a message was handed him from General MacArthur.

It was intended to read: " Your departure from this theater leaves a gap that can only be filled by your return." Chuckling, Halsey noted the transmission error. The word " filled " had come out " fouled."

[Chapter 19]

# Victory!

AFTER A MONTH on leave Halsey returned to duty to a temporary assignment in Washington. At the White House, with Mrs. Halsey present, President Roosevelt awarded him a Gold Star in lieu of a third Distinguished Service Medal "for exceptionally meritorious service to the United States as Commander, Third Fleet."

The citation continued in part:

> Admiral Halsey was directly responsible for the great damage inflicted on enemy aerial forces and the destruction of shipping vital to the Japanese in fighting an increasingly defensive war. Under his forceful and inspiring leadership the recovery of the Philippines was painstakingly prepared for, covered and effectively supported during operations which evidenced his daring tactics and the devotion to duty of his gallant command.

During his absence from the Pacific our troops forced entry to Manila from which they had been driven three years before. The Philippines were again free of Japanese control. In March the island of Iwo Jima was finally taken after a bitter assault. Landing operations began April 1 against Okinawa in the Ryukyu group which, with Japan's steady withdrawal, had become her greatest offshore strong point. Thirteen hundred of our ships were involved in the landing and a hundred eighty-two thousand assault troops.

In Europe the vast Allied armies and air fleets under the command of General Eisenhower were forcing Hitler's Nazi regime into collapse. German armies began to break up and on May 7, 1945, German representatives signed an unconditional surrender. The news that World War II on the other side of the globe was ended was received with great enthusiasm by our forces in the Pacific. In this theater, however, the enemy was considered still far from conquered. Battles remained to be fought and more men must die. Estimates of Japan's staying power varied from six months to three years.

Because the *New Jersey* was being overhauled, Halsey returned to sea duty on May 18 aboard the new battleship *Missouri.* He relieved Admiral Spruance and as his four-star flag was hoisted, remarked with satisfaction: "This is a significant day for me. I served in the old *Missouri* forty years ago." His first order was for the sixteen-inch guns of the *Mighty Mo* to bombard Japanese forces on Okinawa.

During Third Fleet's support of the Okinawa fighting, *kamikazes* had showered destruction on our ships, especially picket destroyers and destroyer escorts whose AA lacked density to shoot them all down. This occurred, Spruance explained grimly, because his role of supporting land operations gave enemy air power the offensive. Halsey chafed at finding himself also tied to troop movements and with his usual dislike for any defensive position argued that it was costly and unprofitable. He kept prodding MacArthur's staff to bend greater efforts to capture enemy airfields and to install more radar ashore. Both would relieve our picket ships.

Meanwhile, he moved partially to the offensive with diversionary air strikes against Kyushu until another of the many typhoons common in these seas cut the series short. In this storm the cruiser *Pittsburgh*'s entire bow was wrenched off, thirty-two other ships were damaged, and a hundred forty-two planes were destroyed.

On a visit to Manila, Halsey found its harbor crowded with

sunken enemy vessels. During the Third's many strikes from September to January its score had been reckoned at a hundred twenty enemy ships sunk, but the harbor showed almost six hundred. Not all were credited to the Third Fleet, though it could claim a large share.

The eighty-two-day Okinawa campaign ended June 21. The two top enemy commanders, Generals Ushimajima and Cho were found to have committed hara-kiri. Action after that consisted in mopping up pockets of Japanese who, as usual, insisted on dying for the Emperor. With Okinawa's fall, a major land and naval phase of the Pacific war was brought to a successful conclusion.

The final phase began July 1 when the Third Fleet sortied from Leyte. Targets were Tokyo and Japan's other principal industrial cities.

Careful preparations were made for attacks on the home empire because it was believed to be bristling with defenses. B-29 bombers made a reconnaissance of Hokkaido and northern Honshu islands. Navy B-24's, guarded by P-51 fighters, photographed Tokyo. When the aircraft carriers neared the coast, every ship was on double alert and seven of our submarines roved ahead to act as lifeguards for splashed pilots. At the first enemy submarine alarm a destroyer full speed on collision course sliced her bow through a whale. Confusion multiplied as porpoises, drifting logs, and the large glass balls Japanese fishermen use to buoy their nets inspired depth charges and constant gunfire. Actual enemy resistance proved so small as to be astonishing.

During our strike not one Japanese plane took the air to object. AA was light and military targets few, but some hangars and other installations were hit and a hundred nine planes on the ground were chewed up, with another two hundred thirty-one damaged. The fleet moved up the coast, pausing for strikes where targets offered.

To reach the important coal and steel city of Muroran on

southern Hokkaido the invaders had to enter a bay. Landlocked, they were in plain sight of shore for three hours. The *Mighty Mo* opened fire at twenty-eight thousand yards as she advanced and pitched a thousand tons of shells ashore, after which came an aerial strike. It took the task force another three hours to retire to sea, but all that plain exposure to the enemy brought only AA fire at our small spotter planes.

Obviously, Japan was no longer bristling with defense.

Hokkaido offered numerous inviting targets of railroads, coastwise shipping, industries, and air facilities. In a two-day attack eighty-four locomotives were destroyed and seventy-one thousand tons of shipping sunk — all to only token resistance. Another strike at Tokyo found AA fire had become heavier, but still there were few defending planes.

Up and down the coasts of Rising Sun Land paraded the Third, blasting with heavy guns, then mounting air strikes to bomb and strafe war industries. Bad weather almost every other day held down the total damage. Attention turned to the Inland Sea area with strikes against airfields and the great Kure Naval Base. Everywhere resistance was feeble.

By the end of July it was apparent that the Japanese Navy had almost ceased to exist. Of twelve battleships only the *Nagato* at Yokosuka was still afloat, too damaged to use. Of twenty-five aircraft carriers, five still floated but were damaged. Of eighteen heavy cruisers, two still existed at Singapore, both damaged, and there remained only two of twenty-two light cruisers. Five destroyers of a hundred seventy-seven still were operational.

Because of diminishing evidence of the enemy air fleet, it was suspected that several hundred planes were being hoarded for a desperate attack on Okinawa. This possibility sent Halsey's Third again to bomb and strafe Hokkaido and Honshu islands. Nearly four hundred planes were destroyed or damaged. Such was the Fleet's contempt for enemy resistance that our bombardment of Kamaishi was staged at an hour convenient

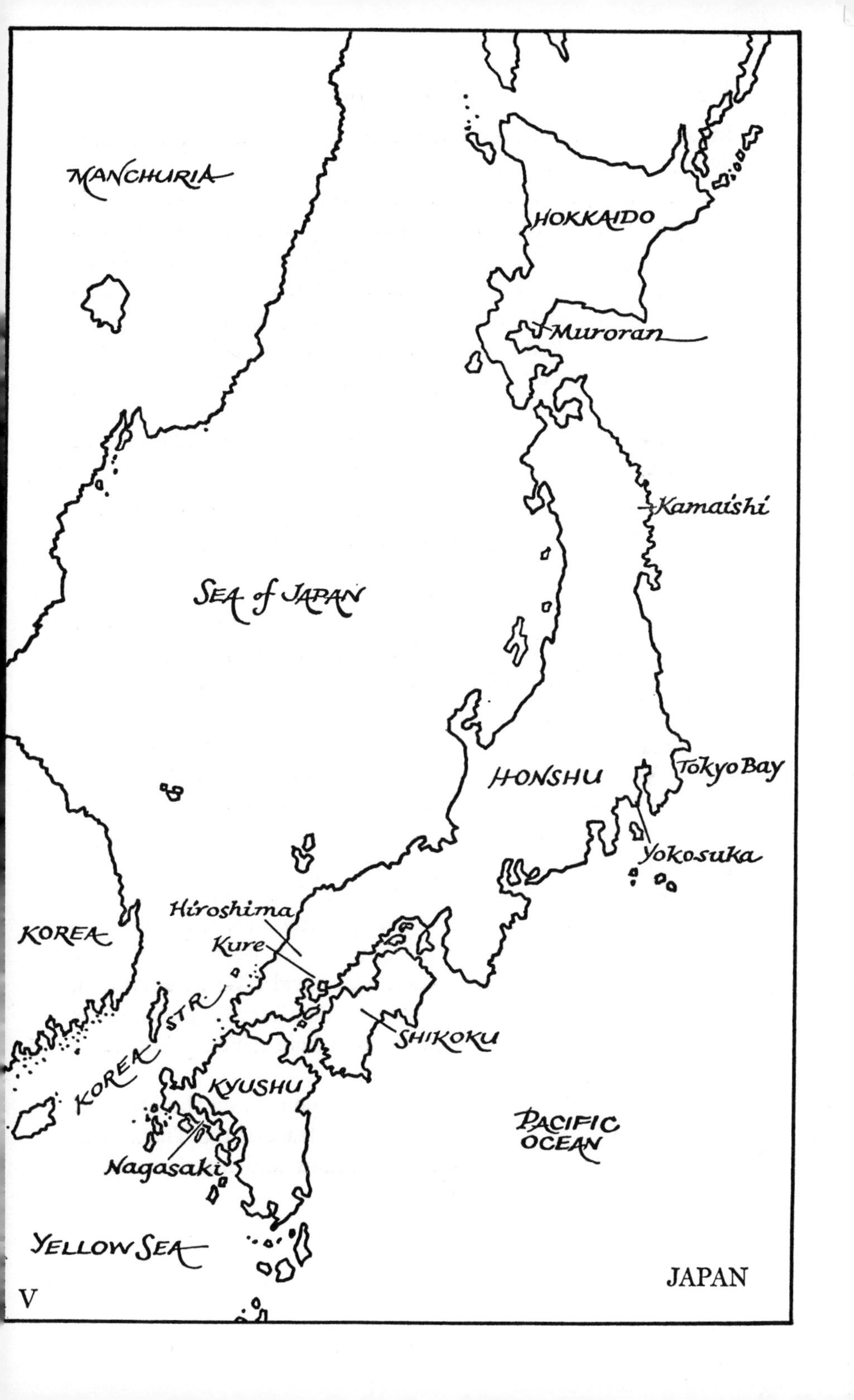
MANCHURIA
HOKKAIDO
Muroran
Kamaishi
SEA of JAPAN
HONSHU
Tokyo Bay
Yokosuka
Hiroshima
Kure
KOREA
KOREA STR.
SHIKOKU
KYUSHU
PACIFIC OCEAN
Nagasaki
YELLOW SEA
JAPAN
V

for Americans to hear on their radios six to nine thousand miles away.

Since mid-July CINCPAC had forbidden Halsey to permit any part of his forces within fifty miles of certain cities. The interdict puzzled him until a representative of CINCPAC arrived with word of the atomic bomb. Bad weather delayed its drop until August 6 on Hiroshima and later on Nagasaki, with results that shocked not only Japan but the world. Now Russia entered the war against Japan, lending psychological but no actual military support. On the tenth the *Missouri's* communications watch officer brought Admirals Carney and Halsey, in flag plot, an intercepted radio announcement:

> Through the Swiss government, Japan states that she is willing to accept Allied surrender ultimatum issued at Potsdam, provided they can keep their Emperor.

The men studied the report. Did it mean the war was over?

"Not for me," Bill Halsey snapped. "Nobody has given me the order to quit. We'll keep up business as usual."

He realized that if the war did soon end, the Third Fleet was the only military group with power and position to enforce the Allies' will until occupation troops could arrive. The thought made him rub his hands in anticipation. Of all United States armor, it would be his proud Third Fleet that actually took Japan into custody!

Quickly he set about organizing a landing force. It consisted of a regiment of Marines, four naval battalions, and five more in reserve, all field-equipped. Commanders were briefed how to take control of the air station and naval base at Yokosuka, how to man enemy vessels, how to demilitarize installations and to air-drop supplies to camps that held Allied prisoners of war.

Messages that immediately began to pour in on the *Missouri* proved that these would be almost the least of the Third's duties on an emergency basis. Instructions and queries arrived concerning military government ashore, landing craft, whole blood, post-office ships, staff cars, interpreters, protocol of official visits, housing, sanitation, and a score of other subjects. They plunged Fleet staff members into new mazes of planning.

But the war was not over. Halsey ordered Admiral McCain to continue the routine of preparing the next air strike against Tokyo.

Another news intercept stated that the American Secretary of State had accepted the surrender of Japan, provided that the Supreme Allied Commander rule Japan through the authority of the Emperor. Although this was not specifically official, Halsey and his advisers began to feel reluctant to attack an enemy in process of yielding. But Admiral Carney argued that no armistice had been declared and no cease-fire order received from COMINCH or CINCPAC. The Japanese never had been trustworthy, he reminded. They should not be trusted now.

" You are absolutely right," Halsey declared.

McCain warned his task force:

KEEP ALERT FOR TRICKS AND BANZAI ATTACKS X THE WAR IS NOT OVER YET X THE NIPS MAY BE PLAYING THEIR NATIONAL GAME OF JUDO, WAITING UNTIL WE ARE CLOSE AND UNWARY

As soon as a delaying typhoon curved away harmlessly Task Force 38 carriers began their run shoreward to the launching point. Before the planes could take off, CINCPAC ordered the strike postponed. Minutes later CINCPAC canceled that order and the operation proceeded. Over the following few hours 38's strikes reduced Japan's air power by another four hundred twenty-two planes. The next day was devoted to refueling and the day after, still lacking any announcement of peace, our attacks resumed.

A flight of one hundred and three planes struck Tokyo and was on its way back to the carriers. Another winging after it was only five minutes from target. Decks were being spotted for a third flight when the signal came:

From: CINCPAC
To: COMTHIRDFLEET
AIR ATTACK WILL BE SUSPENDED X ACKNOWLEDGE

The planes on the decks were ordered held. The second flight was ordered to turn back, but some pilots believed the order an enemy trick and refused to obey until it was authenticated twice.

Was the war over — or only suspended?

On the morning of August 15, 1945, Bill Halsey sat sipping coffee in the *Missouri's* wardroom when Air Operations Officer Douglas Moulton burst in waving a message. "Admiral, here she is!"

Four years before aboard the *Enterprise* Moulton had brought him the first word of the Pearl Harbor raid. "Both times," Halsey noted, chuckling, "Doug caught me at breakfast."

For a moment it was difficult to believe that the war actually was ended. Halsey's first reaction to the news was a half-dazed exclamation, "Victory!" His second was realization that he need never again order men into combat likely to cost their lives. Third came humble gratitude for the honor of being commander of the United States Third Fleet on this historic day.

He read and reread the message. It was a transcript of President Truman's official announcement that the war was over.

Halsey yelled, "*Yippee!*" He pounded the backs of men nearby and was glad to have them pound his. The *Mighty Mo* ran up the "Well-done" flag. Third Fleet ships held down their whistle cords for a full minute of sound. Aviation mechanics and AA gunners waltzed on the decks, and officers and seamen hugged each other, clapped each others' shoulders, and shook hands with all comers.

But as the first glow of jubilation moderated, Halsey found

that his forty years of suspicions of Japanese had not been fully erased. He ordered that bombers and torpedo planes be stowed on hangar decks and that flight decks be spotted with armed fighters. A strong air patrol was thrown aloft lest some *kamikaze* make a last try to win honor for his ancestors.

Fifteen minutes later an air-patrol pilot called from the sky: "Tallyho. One bandit diving!" A pause. The same voice reported, "Splash one Judy."

At 1300, Halsey made a broadcast to his fleet. After congratulating his crews, he warned: "Now that the fighting has ended there must be no letdown. There must be watchful waiting." As if to bear out his words, at 1303 air patrol shot down a Zeke and a Judy and at 1313 another Judy, and at 1335 a destroyer's AA shot down still another Judy. Because of Japan's wrecked communications it is probable that these enemy pilots were not aware that hostilities had officially ceased.

Staff officers of the Third Fleet compiled the score for its two arduous campaigns.

| | |
|---|---:|
| *Planes destroyed or damaged* | 10,355 |
| *Warships sunk* | 130 |
| *Warships probably sunk* | 90 |
| *Warships damaged* | 150 |
| *Merchant vessels sunk* | 1,000 |

The great Third Fleet lay at anchor that sunny morning in Tokyo Bay. All big guns were loaded, manned, and trained on targets ashore. Flight decks of the carriers cruising a few miles at sea were lined with fighter planes cocked for takeoff at the slightest hint of treachery. Over the bay and over the city, with brooding Fujiyama in the distance, droned other planes maintaining complete command of the skies.

The day of formal surrender was September 2, 1945. At 0710 accredited correspondents and photographers filed up the *Missouri*'s boarding stairs. Arriving after them were Navy, Army, Marine, and various Allied representatives. Admiral Nimitz was piped aboard, followed by his staff, then General MacArthur, followed by his.

Halsey's four stars now flew from the nearby battleship *Iowa* out of courtesy to Admiral Nimitz who, as the senior officer present afloat, had his flag at the aftermast of the *Mighty Mo.* General MacArthur's flag soon rippled beside it.

There was another flag aloft, one that to every American seemed to outshine all others. This one had been flown from the flagship of Commodore Perry in almost this identical anchorage. He had come to Japan in 1854 in friendship. Now Washington had sent his flag back across the Pacific by special messenger, by its display to indicate hope for renewed friendship between the two nations.

On the *Missouri's* starboard veranda deck under the glowering muzzles of sixteen-inch rifles of Number Two turret stood a covered table. It bore only two inkwells and pens and two bound copies, desk-blotter size, of the official surrender documents. A straight chair stood on each side of the table. On one side stood General MacArthur and Admiral Nimitz. A short distance from them a group of high Army, Navy, and Marine officers watched with absorbed interest. On the opposite side of the table waited two short, unhappy Japanese envoys, wearing striped trousers, morning coats, top hats, and gloves.

The ceremony began with a brief, earnest address by General MacArthur. Finishing, he pointed to the chair on the other side of the table. "The representatives of the Imperial Japanese Government and of the Imperial Japanese Staff will now come forward and sign."

Halsey's flag log recorded crisply: "0903. Jap envoys told to sign. They did."

First, Foreign Minister Shigemitsu signed in the name of Emperor Hirohito. Then General Umezu signed the documents for the Imperial Staff. This accomplished, they stepped back and watched while on the opposite side of the table General MacArthur signed as Supreme Commander for the Allied

Powers. Admiral Nimitz followed him, then representatives of the Allied nations.

The ceremony was quickly over. With it ended World War II.

A month later Halsey's latest flagship, the battlewagon *South Dakota,* led a triumphant naval parade of fourteen warships single file into San Francisco Bay. The day's great celebration ended, the Navy Department awarded him a Gold Star in lieu of a fourth Distinguished Service Medal. Its accompanying citation outlined his Third Fleet command activities, ending:

> His professional skill and inspiring devotion to the fulfillment of a mission vital to lasting peace reflect the highest credit upon Admiral Halsey and the United States Naval Service.

After his completion of a five weeks' speaking tour of the chief cities of Central and South American countries Halsey returned to duty aboard his flagship at Long Beach. Before leaving Tokyo he had requested retirement as soon as he should be relieved of command. In November he was promoted to be Fleet Admiral, the topmost Navy rank and one attained by only a handful of Americans. His official retirement came April 1, 1947.

As his five-star flag was slowly hauled down from the *South Dakota*'s aftermast for the last time, Bill Halsey, with sadness ringing in his voice, told the ship's company:

> I am terminating a seagoing career of slightly over forty-five years. This is far from a pleasure, but I deem it necessary for men of my age to step aside so that younger men can take over the greatest Navy in the world. . . . You have heard the nation say, "Well done!" I say it to you again and again: "Well done! Well done! Well done!" May you all have happy careers! Godspeed and God bless you!

After twelve years of retirement Fleet Admiral William Frederick Halsey, Jr., one of America's greatest naval heroes, died on August 16, 1959. He lies buried in Arlington National Cemetery.

# Bibliography


Bryan, Joseph, *Aircraft Carrier*. Ballantine Bks, Inc., 1954.

Bryan, Joseph, "Four Star Sea Dog," *Saturday Evening Post*, December 25, 1943; January 1, 1944.

Cant, G., "Bull's Run," *Life*, November 24, 1947.

*Famous American Military Leaders of World War II*. By editors of the *Army Times*. Dodd, Mead & Company, Inc., 1962.

*Generals and the Admirals: Some Leaders of the United States Forces in World War II*. Portraits by T. H. Chamberlain. Biographies by the editors of *Newsweek*. Devin-Adair Company, 1945. 2 vols.

*The Great Sea War: The Story of Naval Action in World War II*, ed. by E. B. Potter and Chester W. Nimitz. Prentice-Hall, Inc., 1960.

Halsey, William F., and Bryan, Joseph, *Admiral Halsey's Story*. Whittlesey House, 1947.

Hamilton, Andrew, "Where Is Task Force 34?" *U.S. Naval Institute Proceedings*, Vol. 86, October, 1960.

Jordan, Ralph Burden, *Born to Fight: The Life of Admiral Halsey*. David McKay Company, Inc., 1946.

Karig, Walter, and Kelley, Welbourn, *Battle Report*, Vol. 1, *Pearl Harbor to Coral Sea*. Farrar & Rinehart, Inc., 1944.

Karig, Walter, Harris, Russel L., and Manson, Frank A., *Battle Report*, Vol. 4, *The End of an Empire*. Rinehart and Co., Inc., 1948.

Karig, Walter, and Purdon, Eric, *Battle Report*, Vol. 3, *Pacific War: Middle Phase*. Rinehart and Co., Inc., 1947.

Morison, Samuel Eliot, *History of U.S. Naval Operations in World War II.* Little, Brown and Company, 1948–1960. Vols. 3, 4, 5, 6, 7, 8, 12, 13, 14.

Prange, Gordon, *Tora, Tora, Tora!* McGraw-Hill Book Company, Inc., 1964.

Roupe, R. H., "Halsey's Famous Signals," *U.S. Naval Institute Proceedings,* Vol. 77, August, 1951.

Stafford, Edward P., *The Big "E": The Story of the U.S.S. Enterprise.* Random House, Inc., 1962.

Tregaskis, Richard William, *Guadalcanal Diary.* Random House, Inc., 1943.

## Biography of Lawrence A. Keating

Lawrence A. Keating's hometown is La Grange, Illinois. After a period of reporting, he became a salesman in Chicago. But writing was his great interest, and he left his position to win in three years a journalism degree at Marquette University, Milwaukee. For a year he worked on a Detroit paper, but because of failing health, was forced to be inactive two years. Returning to the typewriter at the rate of ten minutes daily while still confined to bed, Keating began a new career as an author. To date he has published twenty-eight books and more than six hundred magazine articles and stories, including a monthly series that so far has run eight years.

During World War II, Keating served the American Red Cross as Assistant Director of Public Information, Midwestern Area, his work taking him to all service camps in seventeen states. " I learned not to be afraid of top sergeants, generals, or admirals," Keating said.

He lives in Milwaukee, where he maintains a downtown office for his writing; he teaches part-time at Marquette University and the University of Wisconsin, Milwaukee. Mr. Keating is well-known for his vigorous true-to-life sports stories for young people. He is a member of the Authors' League of America, Inc., and of the Society of Midland Authors.